A Guide to
Aquatic Insects
and
Crustaceans

The Izaak Walton League
of America

STACKPOLE
BOOKS

Published by
STACKPOLE BOOKS
5067 Ritter Rd.
Mechanicsburg, PA 17055

Printed in the United States of America

10 9 8 7 6 5 4 3 2 1

This is a revised and updated edition of the book *Monitor's Guide to Aquatic Macroinvertebrates*, originally published in 1992 by the Izaak Walton League of America.

Staff Contributors

Second edition text	Kami Watson-Ferguson
Editors	Cindy Han, Jason McGarvey, Leah Miller
Appendices	Gwyn Rowland, Casey Williams
First edition text	Loren Kellogg

Illustrations by Daryl Ratajczak
Cover design by Caroline Stover

Library of Congress Cataloging-in-Publication Data

Watson-Ferguson, Kami.
  A guide to aquatic insects and crustaceans / The Izaak Walton League of America ; [text by Kami Watson-Ferguson ; editors, Cindy Han, Jason McGarvey, Leah Miller].
    p. cm.
  Includes bibliographical references and index.
  ISBN-13: 978-0-8117-3245-1 (alk. paper)
  1. Aquatic insects—East (U.S.)—Identification. 2. Crustacea—East (U.S.)—Identification. I. Han, Cindy. II. McGarvey, Jason. III. Miller, Leah. IV. Izaak Walton League of America. V. Title.
QL475.E27W38 2006
595.71760974—dc22

2005037914

Contents

Acknowledgments

We would like to thank those who volunteered their time to review and comment on this guide. Their shared knowledge and comments have greatly contributed to making this guide possible. The Izaak Walton League of America thanks the following people:

- Phil Emmling, Environmental Chemistry and Technology Department, University of Wisconsin-Madison
- Phillip Ray Gibson, Director of Research and Community Outreach, Environmental Leadership Center, Warren Wilson College
- Stephen Hiner, Department of Entomology, College of Agriculture and Life Sciences, Virginia Polytechnic Institute and State University
- Chris Riggert, Stream Team Biologist, Fisheries Division, Stream Unit, Missouri Department of Conservation
- J. Reese Voshell Jr., Ph.D., Department of Entomology, College of Agriculture and Life Sciences, Virginia Polytechnic Institute and State University

Introduction

In 1992, the Izaak Walton League of America, one of the nation's oldest and most respected community-based conservation organizations, published the first edition of its *Monitor's Guide to Aquatic Macroinvertebrates*. This guide was written to help volunteers monitor the quality of their local streams and rivers using the League's Save Our Streams method of biological monitoring. Using this method, the general health of the water can be determined by measuring the amount of certain aquatic insects and crustaceans. The *Monitor's Guide to Aquatic Macroinvertebrates* lists these organisms, includes descriptions for identifying them, and provides information regarding their sensitivity to pollution.

Now in its second edition—fully updated with a new publisher and a new title—*A Guide to Aquatic Insects and Crustaceans* is intended to assist volunteers monitor biological water quality. It is also aimed at those who are interested in aquatic macroinvertebrates for other purposes, such as fly-fishermen trying to match hatches, naturalists exploring local waters, and educators and students.

Whatever your interest, this guide will help you learn more about the insects and crustaceans that live in freshwater streams, lakes, and rivers. Within these pages, you will discover an excellent resource for biological monitoring as well as a helpful tool to assist you in your underwater exploration and discovery.

Get curious, look closer, and have fun.

The Izaak Walton League of America

Founded in 1922, the Izaak Walton League of America is dedicated to common-sense conservation that protects America's outdoor heritage, relying on solution-oriented conservation, education, and the promotion of outdoor recreation for the benefit of our citizens. The League has more than 40,000 members and supporters in 21 state divisions, and more than 300 local chapters in 32 states.

At the community level, League members engage in hands-on conservation action, such as monitoring streams, protecting and restoring wetlands, picking up litter, and planting trees. At the regional and national levels, the League works toward better laws, funding for conservation, and public education. For more than 30 years, the League has developed innovative watershed education programs through Save Our Streams and Protect Our Wetlands.

Citizen action at the community level makes a difference. We invite you to become an active steward of our nation's streams, rivers, and wetlands. To help you, the League has developed a variety of handbooks and videos about stream monitoring, habitat restoration, and wetland stewardship. This is just one of the many tools designed to assist your watershed stewardship program. If you would like to learn more about our educational resources, League chapters active in your community, or how to get started as a watershed steward, please contact the League at (800) BUG-IWLA or visit online at www.iwla.org.

Izaak Walton League of America
707 Conservation Lane
Gaithersburg, MD 20878
Phone: (301) 548-0150
Fax: (301) 548-0146
Assistance with watershed conservation questions:
    (800) BUG-IWLA (284-4952)
E-mail: sos@iwla.org
Website: www.iwla.org

Water Quality Monitoring

Water quality monitoring is the measurement or observation of a waterway over time. It allows people to assess water conditions and to determine if waters can support aquatic life, or whether they are safe enough for swimming and fishing. Monitoring data can be used to inform and educate your relatives, friends, and neighbors about the condition of your local streams. It can help establish a baseline for the water quality of a stream, since data for many streams is sparse or nonexistent. Monitoring data can also be used to identify pollution problems, determine whether pollution regulations are being followed, and gauge whether enhancement efforts are successful.

The Izaak Walton League's Save Our Streams program uses biological monitoring of aquatic macroinvertebrates because it provides an effective, easy-to-understand method of determining if a stream has been affected by pollution. Aquatic macroinvertebrates are organisms that live in water for all or part of their lives, are large enough to be seen without the aid of a microscope ("macro"), and do not have backbones ("invertebrate"). Benthic macroinvertebrates live in the benthos, or stream bottom, and include insect larvae, adult insects, aquatic worms, crustaceans, and mollusks. The Izaak Walton League measures benthic macroinvertebrates in streams to determine water quality; they can also be monitored in wetlands. If the water quality is generally poor, or if a pollution event occurred within the past several months, it may be reflected through a decline in the macroinvertebrate population. This book includes only macroinvertebrates that live in water for at least part of their life cycle.

The Save Our Streams biological monitoring method was developed in 1983 by the Ohio Department of Natural Resources and the Izaak Walton League of America. The simple, reliable technique is based on the fact that different groups of stream macroinvertebrates have different tolerances to pollution, and therefore can serve as useful indicators of water quality. They may live from several weeks to many years in the same area of a stream and directly depend on adequate habitat and water quality for survival. As a result, macroinvertebrates can indicate pollution from cumulative or multiple sources. For monitoring streams, the League identifies three types of macroinvertebrates based on their sensitivity to pollution: sensitive, less sensitive, and tolerant. The Save Our Streams method involves collecting a sample of macroinvertebrates from the stream, identifying the organisms, and rating the water quality. Water quality ratings of excellent, good, fair, and poor are based on the pollution tolerance levels of the organisms found and the diversity of organisms in the sample. A stream with excellent water quality should support organisms from all three tolerance groups. If you are interested in using the Save Our Streams method, review the instructions in Appendix A.

Aquatic macroinvertebrates can also be categorized into five main "functional feeding groups" that are named after the feeding patterns of different species:

- *Shredders* feed on coarse organic materials such as leaves and aquatic plants. They play an important role in breaking down large pieces of organic material to a size that can be used by other macroinvertebrates. Shredders include some types of stonefly and caddisfly larvae, sowbugs, and scuds.
- *Collectors* feed on fine pieces of organic material such as leaf fragments, bacteria, and waste from other organisms. Collectors are often further divided into filtering collectors and gathering collectors. Filtering collectors such as clams are able to move water with their bodies to gather food. Another example is the common net-spinning caddisfly, which spins a silklike web to strain water as it flows downstream. Gathering collectors such as mayfly and caddisfly larvae, nonbiting midges, and aquatic worms will eat the organic materials that have dropped out of the water column and settled along the bottom.
- *Scrapers* graze on algae attached to stones and other surfaces. Many of these organisms have flattened bodies to help them cling to their feeding surfaces while water rushes over them. Scrapers include water pennies, limpets, snails, net-winged midge larvae, and flat-headed mayfly larvae.
- *Piercers* utilize specialized mouthparts to extract the insides of either a plant or an animal. The less common piercer-herbivores penetrate the tissues of aquatic plants to extract the liquid insides. Piercer-herbivores such as micro caddisflies have small heads that can be inserted into holes they have nibbled in plants.

Piercer-carnivores are more common. They subdue and kill their prey by injecting poison and digestive enzymes, which reduce the internal organs to a liquid that they then suck out. The predaceous diving beetle is an excellent example of a piercer-carnivore.

• *Engulfer-predators* feed on other living aquatic animals such as fish and invertebrates. Predatory organisms include dobsonfly and hellgrammite larvae, fishfly larvae, dragonfly, stonefly, and watersnipe fly larvae.

Although the Save Our Streams monitoring method is based entirely on pollution tolerance, the macroinvertebrate feeding patterns observed in the course of biological monitoring can provide insight into the nature of stream disturbances. For example, increased proportions of scrapers may indicate nutrient runoff, while increased numbers of collectors may show organic enrichment. Some biological monitoring programs choose to include this information in their data in addition to their findings based on tolerance. However, variables such as season, temperature, and stream location must be taken into account.

Chemical testing can also be very important for understanding the quality or health of a stream, but this technique often supplies only limited information, such as nutrient or dissolved oxygen concentration. In addition, equipment can be very expensive and monitoring may be time consuming, often requiring weekly or hourly sampling. Regular macroinvertebrate monitoring, with samples taken four to six times a year, can indicate problems that may not easily be detected by chemical testing and can reveal pollution problems that may no longer be evident in current water samples (for example, a chemical spill that washes downstream). Measuring the biological health of the stream is a fast, effective way to determine its overall condition. Chemical testing may be used in conjunction with biological monitoring to learn more about the specific causes of water pollution.

Using this Guide

This guide was originally created to aid in the field identification of aquatic insects, crustaceans, and other aquatic macroinvertebrates of the eastern United States. As a result, emphasis was placed on those common to this region. It should be noted, however, that almost all of these organisms are found across North America, so the characteristics and identification techniques included here will apply to other areas of the country and Canada as well. It is possible, however, that some of the macroinvertebrates in this book might not be found in your area. In addition, this guide covers only those macroinvertebrates that spend at least part of their lives under water. There are other organisms that may be found infrequently in aquatic environments; for this reason, a source list of additional macroinvertebrate keys and guides is included for further reference.

There are two sections to help identify macroinvertebrates. The first is the Key to Aquatic Macroinvertebrate Groups, which helps you determine a category for a given macroinvertebrate. The second is titled Aquatic Macroinvertebrates, which lists distinguishing characteristics for each group (class, order, or family) and subgroup (if applicable). It also includes information on life cycles and the most likely habitats.

To identify a macroinvertebrate, follow these steps:

1. Use the Key to Aquatic Macroinvertebrate Groups to determine the group to which the organism belongs.
2. Turn to the page number listed after the name of the group. Read the detailed description found on that page.
3. If you've made a mistake in identifying the organism, it should be evident when you read the group characteristics. If this is the case, read the section labeled "Similar Aquatic Macroinvertebrates" and turn to the appropriate group section. If none of the descriptions there match the organism in question, return to the Key and carefully reconsider each entry for possible alternatives.

Remember that although group characteristics will apply to subgroups, the reverse will not necessarily be true.

Defining Levels of Classification

Scientists divide the living world into groups according to the International Code of Zoological Nomenclature. These divisions progress from general (kingdom) to more specific (species). In this book, macroinvertebrate groups are listed by common names; however, information about taxonomy appears in parentheses next to the common name. Classifications in this book are consistent with *Ecology and Classification of North American Freshwater Invertebrates* (Thorp and Covich, 1991).

The hierarchy as determined by the International Code of Zoological Nomenclature is:

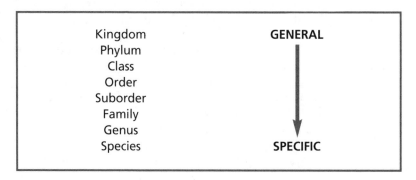

In this guide, we identify macroinvertebrates primarily down to the level order, and down to family when necessary. This level of identification can be done without a scientific background or the use of equipment such as microscopes. It is widely used by volunteer groups and allows them to gather the most accurate data.

Key to Aquatic Macroinvertebrate Groups

This key is designed to aid in the identification of different stream macroinvertebrates. Called a dichotomous key, it consists of pairs of statements with opposite characteristics. To use this key, start at box 1 and read statements A and B. Then decide which statement best describes the organism and go to the next indicated box. Repeat this procedure until the macroinvertebrate group and page number are identified.

The information contained on the indicated pages should further support this identification. If the organism has been misidentified, read the section on similar macroinvertebrates and check the descriptions of these to find a match. If no match is found, return to this key and reconsider each appropriate statement.

If the macroinvertebrate is found in a portable case (usually constructed of pebbles, sand, or pieces of leaves or other vegetation), it should be carefully removed. In addition, it may be helpful to wash or remove any debris from the organism. You might need a simple magnifying glass to identify some of the characteristics in question.

For definitions of terms, please see the Glossary.

1

A. Has segmented (jointed) legs.

Go to box 2

B. Does not have segmented (jointed) legs.   *Go to box 17*

2

A. Has only six segmented (jointed) legs.   *Go to box 3*

B. Has more than six segmented (jointed) legs. *Go to box 14*

3

A. Body elongated (longer than it is wide) and legs not concealed beneath body.

Go to box 4

B. Body disk- or oval-shaped and flat.

WATER PENNY LARVA *(page 30)*

4

A. Two or three distinct tails that may appear hairlike, webbed, or broad paddle shaped.

Go to box 5

B. No tails, or a tail consisting of a single long filament, or consisting of hooked tails, which may or may not have short filaments.

Go to box 7

5

A. Two or three hairlike tails (may appear webbed); platelike, filamentous, or feathery gills along sides of abdomen.

MAYFLY LARVA *(page 20)*

B. Two or three hairlike or paddle-shaped tails; no gills along sides of abdomen.

Go to box 6

6

A. Two hairlike tails; two antennae; no gills along sides of abdomen.

STONEFLY LARVA *(page 19)*

B. Three broad paddle-shaped tails (sometimes hairlike); no gills along sides of abdomen.

DAMSELFLY LARVA *(page 27)*

7

A. Abdomen is hardened; body is plated or skin is hardened.   *Go to box 8*

B. Abdomen is soft—not hardened or plated.   *Go to box 9*

8

A. Wide abdomen; large eyes; large scooplike lower lip that covers bottom of mouth.

DRAGONFLY LARVA *(page 27)*

B. Whole body is hardened and stiff; tail may have opening with tiny hooks and filaments extending.

RIFFLE BEETLE LARVA *(page 29)*

9

A. Fleshy or thin filament extending from sides of abdomen in pairs, one on each side of each abdominal segment.

Go to box 10

B. No pairs of fleshy appendages extending from sides of body; abdomen is fleshy.

Go to box 13

10

A. Fleshy or branched gill tufts under abdomen; a pair of unjointed prolegs on the back end, each with a pair of claws.

DOBSONFLY LARVA *(page 25)*

B. No gill tufts under abdomen; fleshy or thin filaments extending from the sides of the abdomen.

Go to box 11

11

A. No gill tufts under abdomen (smooth); short forked tail; fleshy or thin filaments extending from sides of the abdomen.

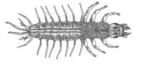

FISHFLY LARVA *(page 25)*

B. No gill tufts under abdomen; abdomen either ends in a single long tail filament or comes to a point.

Go to box 12

12

A. Single long tail filament; no gill tufts under abdomen.

ALDERFLY LARVA *(page 25)*

B. Abdomen comes to a point (with four very tiny hooks extending); no gill tufts under abdomen.

WHIRLIGIG BEETLE LARVA *(page 31)*

13

A. Two small hooks on forked back end (may be hidden, feathery, or branched taillike structures); underside of abdomen may have fluffy gills; may be hiding in a case made of sand and/or plant material.

CADDISFLY LARVA *(page 22)*

B. Abdomen has pairs of caterpillarlike legs extending from abdomen; segmented body may be smooth or covered with filaments.

AQUATIC PYRALID MOTH LARVA   *(page 34)*

14

A. Body resembles a lobster or shrimp.

Go to box 15

B. Flattened in appearance; walks slowly; may look like a "pillbug" or "roly-poly."

SOWBUG *(page 41)*

15

A. Body resembles a lobster or shrimp and has thin plates forming a fan-shaped tail.

Go to box 16

B. Shrimplike body with no tail or tiny filaments extending from back end; body is higher than it is wide; swims quickly on its side.

SCUD *(page 40)*

16

A. Lobsterlike body with ten legs, including two large claws.

CRAYFISH *(page 39)*

B. Shrimplike body, higher than it is wide. Pincers (claws) are not greatly enlarged.

FRESHWATER SHRIMP *(page 40)*

17

A. Has a distinct head.

Go to box 18

B. Does not have a distinct head.

Go to box 22

18

A. With distinct head and one or more very tiny non-jointed (unsegmented) leglike appendages.

Go to box 19

B. With distinct head and no legs or leglike appendages.

Go to box 21

19

A. Very tiny (under ½ inch) body that may appear inchwormlike or widened at one end.

Go to box 20

B. Distinct segmented body; suckers on each segment along the center of the underside.

NET-WINGED MIDGE LARVA *(page 39)*

20

A. Both ends about the same width, with a very tiny pair of legs under head and a very tiny pair under abdomen.

MIDGE *(page 36)*

B. Body widens at back end (bowling pin shaped); dark (usually black) head.

BLACK FLY LARVA *(page 36)*

21

A. Body is stiff with hard skin; head is set off from body; body is wider at upper end and tapers to a point; body may have bristles or hairs.

SOLDIER FLY LARVA *(page 38)*

B. Flattened, unsegmented, wormlike body; usually has distinct eye spots; has gliding movement.

PLANARIAN *(page 46)*

22

A. Body has distinct legs or leglike appendages; no visible head. *Go to box 23*

B. Body has no legs or leglike appendages; no visible head. *Go to box 24*

23

A. Two feathered horns on posterior; caterpillar-like legs.

**WATERSNIPE
FLY LARVA** *(page 35)*

B. Variable number of short fleshy extensions from posterior; extensions not feathered; caterpillarlike legs.

**DANCE
FLY LARVA** *(page 37)*

24

A. Body without hard shell.

Go to box 25

B. Body with hard shell or shells.

Go to box 28

25

A. Wormlike body that may or may not have suckers at each end.

Go to box 26

B. Soft, plump, caterpillarlike body.

Go to box 27

26

A. Segmented body with suckers at each end; swimming or end-to-end movement.

LEECH *(page 44)*

B. Long, segmented body; earthworm- or threadlike.

AQUATIC WORM *(page 45)*

27

A. Caterpillarlike body with fleshy, fingerlike extensions from one end.

CRANE FLY LARVA *(page 34)*

B. Caterpillarlike body, tapered to a point at both ends.

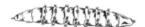

HORSE FLY and DEER FLY LARVA *(page 38)*

28

A. Single spiraled, coiled, or hat-shaped shell.

Go to box 30

B. Body enclosed within two hinged shells.

CLAM and MUSSEL *(page 43)*

29

A. Has platelike cover over opening; when spire is pointed up and shell opening faces you, shell usually opens on your right.

GILLED SNAIL *(page 42)*

B. Does not have platelike cover over opening; shell may be spiraled, coiled in one plane, or domeshaped. If coiled, when spire is pointed up and shell opening faces you, shell usually opens on your left.

Go to box 30

30

A. Shell is spiraled and does not have platelike cover over opening; when spire is pointing up and shell opening faces you, shell usually opens on your left.

LUNGED SNAIL *(page 42)*

B. Shell coiled in one plane or domeshaped, and opening does not have platelike cover.

LIMPET *(page 42)*

Aquatic Macroinvertebrates

Insects: Class *Insecta*

■ **Stoneflies** (Order *Plecoptera*)

Stonefly larvae are one of the most pollution-sensitive groups of macroinvertebrates. Typically, stonefly larvae are found in cool, clean streams with high levels of dissolved oxygen. All of the more than 600 species of stoneflies found in North America have aquatic larvae, and all but one species, the *Utacapnia* found deep within Lake Tahoe, are terrestrial as adults. Larval development in the aquatic environment usually takes between three months to three years, and during the year, stonefly larvae of different species hatch into adults at different times.

Stonefly larvae are mostly either engulfer-predators or shredders. (See Water Quality Monitoring for definitions of feeding behaviors.) Sometimes, as very young larvae, they are gathering collectors, and their feeding behavior changes with growth.

Generally, stoneflies have flattened bodies with legs that end in two hooks, which allow them to hold bottom in fast moving currents.

Stoneflies are distinguished by:
- two antennae that are several times longer than their head.
- two hairlike tails.
- gill tufts that can be found where the legs join the body. There are no gills on the rear half of the body.
- three pairs of segmented legs (six legs total) on middle section of body, with two claws at the end of each leg.
- body length: ½ inch to 1½ inch.

Similar Aquatic Macroinvertebrates

Stonefly larvae are similar to mayfly larvae; however, mayflies have platelike or feathery gill tufts along the sides of their abdomen,

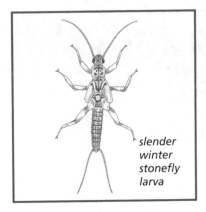

slender
winter
stonefly
larva

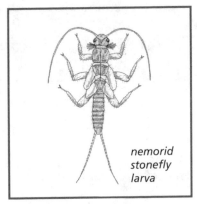

nemorid
stonefly
larva

and stoneflies have none (stonefly larvae may have gill tufts between the legs on the thorax). More noticeably, mayfly larvae usually have three tails (although a few have two), while stoneflies have only two hairlike tails. Also, the antennae of mayfly larvae are often only half as long as those of stonefly larvae. Furthermore, mayfly larvae have only one hook at the end of each leg, while stonefly larvae have two hooks.

Damselfly larvae can also look like stoneflies, but the former have three (not two) oar-shaped tails and short antennae.

■ Mayflies (Order *Ephemeroptera*)

All of the approximately 700 species of mayflies have aquatic larvae and a relatively short-lived terrestrial adult stage. The larval development period depends on species and local climate but can last from two weeks to two years. Mayflies of the same species

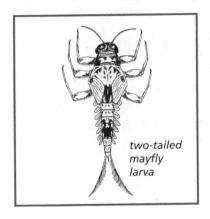

two-tailed
mayfly
larva

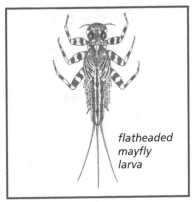

flatheaded
mayfly
larva

often emerge together from the water in a short time frame. This "hatch" may be observed emerging from the stream or as a swirling mass flying above it. Because of the large number of different species and varying life cycles, mayfly larvae can be observed in a healthy stream at any time of year.

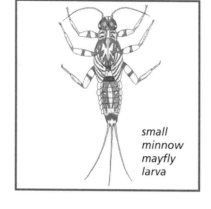

small minnow mayfly larva

Mayfly larvae can be found in a variety of habitats, including exposed rock surfaces in fast current or buried in soft stream bottoms. Generally, mayfly larvae are confined to streams with high levels of dissolved oxygen and good water quality.

Mayfly larvae are distinguished by:

- platelike, filamentous, or feathery gills along the sides or top of the rear half of the abdomen. Gills can be either brown, cream, or white. One family of mayflies, *Baetiscidae*, has gills hidden under a hard body plate, but these mayflies can be distinguished by their three tails.
- three (sometimes two) long hairlike tails on the abdomen that extend from the body at the same level (flat with ground). The tails may appear webbed.
- three pairs of segmented legs (six legs total) on the middle section of the body.
- a flattened or rounded body.

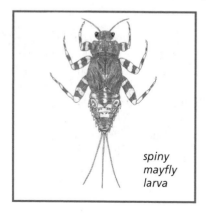

spiny mayfly larva

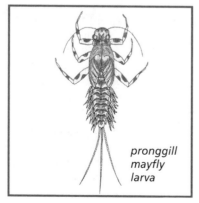

pronggill mayfly larva

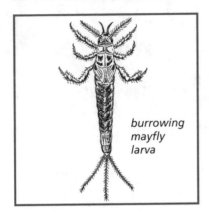

burrowing
mayfly
larva

armored
mayfly
larva

- one claw at the end of each leg (rarely no claws).
- body length: ½ inch to 1 inch.

Similar Aquatic Macroinvertebrates

Mayfly larvae may be distinguished from stonefly larvae by the presence of platelike or feathery gill tufts along the sides of the abdomen. In addition, mayfly larvae usually have three hair-like tails and very short antennae (usually shorter than head length).

Damselfly larvae can also be similar to mayfly larvae, except damselfly larvae have no abdominal gills and have three broad oar-shaped tails that extend from the posterior of the damselfly in a tripod formation. These tails are the damselfly larvae's gills. They extend from the posterior of the abdomen and are parallel to the ground.

■ Caddisflies (Order *Trichoptera*)

Caddisflies are a large group of organisms that have adapted to many types of aquatic environments. Many caddisfly larvae live inside of casings, which they construct out of different materials such as rocks, sand, gravel, twigs, leaves, or other debris. The larvae glue the materials together using a substance secreted from their labium (silk glands in their lower lip). Often, the methods and materials a caddisfly uses to construct its "house" can be helpful in identifying its taxonomic group. Typically, caddisflies have one generation (hatch) per year, but many have several overlapping generations annually.

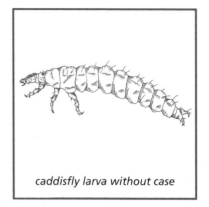

caddisfly larva without case

caddisfly larva with case

Caddisfly larvae are distinguished by:
- casing constructed of sand, gravel, or parts of leaves or twigs.
- three pairs of segmented legs (six legs total) on the upper-middle section of the body with a single claw at each end.
- two small, fleshy extensions at the base of the abdomen, each ending in a single hook.
- filamentous gills present on the underside or end of a caterpillarlike abdomen.
- no antennae usually present; if present, they are very small and inconspicuous.
- characteristic motion (known as the "caddisfly dance") of wiggling back and forth, then up and down in water.
- body or casing length: ½ inch to 1½ inch.

Similar Aquatic Macroinvertebrates

Caddisfly larvae can be confused with dobsonfly larvae, fishfly larvae, alderfly larvae, beetle larvae, aquatic caterpillars, or midge larvae. They can be distinguished by the presence of single hooks on the end of each leg and at both tips of a slightly forked abdomen (dobsonfly and fishfly larvae have a forked tail with two distinct hooks on each fork, and similar-looking beetle larvae have four hooks extending from a single point on the end of the abdomen). In addition, caddisfly larvae do not have long pointed tails (like alderfly larvae), caterpillarlike legs (like aquatic caterpillars or watersnipe larvae), or prolegs on the first segment (like midge larvae).

Like dobsonfly larvae, filamentous gills may be located on the underside of the caddisfly (along its belly). Caddisflies do not, however, have the fleshy or hairlike appendages protruding from the sides of the abdomen that are characteristic of dobsonfly, alderfly, fishfly, or certain beetle larvae. Caddisfly larvae can be distinguished from the riffle beetle larvae by the presence of a fleshy abdomen. Riffle beetle larvae have a hardened, stiff appearance along the entire body. Caddisfly larvae have only a hard covering over the first one, two, or three segments.

☐ Common Net-Spinning Caddisflies (Family *Hydopsychindae*)

Common net-spinning caddisflies are similar in appearance to other caddisflies. They are only found in flowing waters, however, where they are able to catch their food with filter nets constructed of silk spun from their labium. Net-spinning caddisflies also build nearby retreats attached to a rock, where they reside until something is caught in their nets. They are collector-filterers and will consume whatever is caught, including invertebrates, plants, algae, and detritus.

Many species of net-spinning caddisflies can coexist and are often found in larger rivers. They are also often seen where there is a greater flow of detritus in the water column, as well as below dams where algae will grow and then flow from the upstream impairment. Net spinners are more tolerant of water pollution than other types of caddisflies.

Common net-spinning caddisflies are distinguished by:

- color that varies from bright green to dark brown.
- three pairs of segmented legs (six legs total) on the upper-middle section of the body with a single claw at each end.
- two fleshy extensions at the end of the strongly curved abdomen. These extensions have a hairy or feathery appearance and a single hook at each end.
- filamentous gills that may be present on the underside or end of a caterpillarlike abdomen.
- no antennae, or antennae that are very small and inconspicuous.

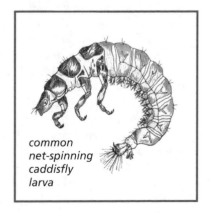

common net-spinning caddisfly larva

- a hard head and a hard, dark plate on all three middle body sections.
- characteristic motion (known as the "caddisfly dance") of wiggling back and forth, then up and down in water.
- body or casing length: up to 1 inch.

Similar Aquatic Macroinvertebrates

Like other caddisfly larvae, common net-spinning caddisfly larvae can be confused with dobsonfly larvae, fishfly larvae, alderfly larvae, beetle larvae, aquatic caterpillars, or midge larvae. Net-spinning caddisfly larvae can be distinguished by the presence of single hooks on the end of each leg and at both tips of a slightly forked abdomen (dobsonfly and fishfly larvae have a forked tail with two distinct hooks on each fork, and similar-looking beetle larvae have four hooks extending from a single point on the end of the abdomen). In addition, caddisfly larvae do not have long pointed tails (like alderfly), caterpillarlike legs (like aquatic caterpillars or water snipe larvae), or prolegs on the first segment (like midge larvae).

Like dobsonfly larvae, filamentous gills may be located on the underside of caddisfly larvae (along its belly). Caddisflies do not, however, have the fleshy or hairlike appendages protruding from the sides of the abdomen that are characteristic of dobsonfly, alderfly, fishfly, or certain beetle larvae. Net-spinning caddisfly larvae can be distinguished from riffle beetle larvae by the presence of a fleshy abdomen. Riffle beetle larvae have a hardened, stiff appearance along the entire body. Caddisfly larvae only have a hard covering over the first one, two, or three segments.

■ Dobsonflies/Hellgrammites, Fishflies, and Alderflies (Order *Megaloptera*)

Fishfly and dobsonfly larvae, also known as hellgrammites, as well as alderfly larvae are aquatic and carnivorous and may bite if not handled carefully. To avoid getting pinched, use tweezers or grasp the larvae directly behind the head. The larval stage generally lasts less than a year, although the stage may sometimes last up to three years. Dobsonflies and fishflies tend to be found in healthy to moderately healthy aquatic environments, while alderflies can be found in a broader range of water quality. The three groups in this order have common traits that distinguish them from other insect larvae.

Dobsonflies, fishflies, and alderflies are distinguished by:

- three pairs of segmented legs (six legs total) on upper-middle section of the body with tiny pincers at the end of each leg.
- abdominal segments with many fleshy, filamentous appendages extending from each side.
- large pincerlike mouthparts.

Two characteristics important for distinguishing between dobsonfly, fishfly, and alderfly larvae are the presence of gill tufts on the underside of the abdomen (underneath the fleshy extensions), and the shape of the tail. The following characteristics will help determine if your specimen is the larva of a dobsonfly, fishfly, or alderfly:

Dobsonfly larvae or hellgrammite (Family *Corydalidae*):
- Eight pairs of pointed appendages along its abdomen.
- Paired cottonlike or filamentous gill tufts located under the abdominal appendages (look like hairy armpits on the underside of the tail section).
- A pair of unjointed prolegs on the posterior, each with a pair of claws.
- Usually dark brown to black in color.
- Body length: ¾ inch to 4 inches.

Fishfly larvae (Family *Corydalidae*):
- No gill tufts underneath the abdomen (smooth underside).
- The posterior is forked with two short, fleshy tails and two hooks on each tail.
- May be lighter in color, a reddish-tan.
- Breathing tubes (may be retracted and not visible) that

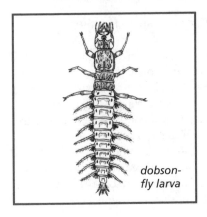

dobson-fly larva

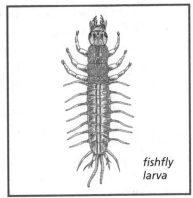

fishfly larva

extend from the top of the abdomen.
- Body length: ¾ inch to 4 inches.

Alderfly larvae (Family *Sialidae*):
- Seven pairs of pointed appendages on the rear half of the body.
- No gill tufts underneath the abdomen (smooth underside).

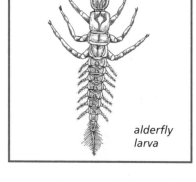

alderfly larva

- Has single-branch tail filament extending straight back.
- May be light colored.
- Body length: up to 1½ inch.

Similar Aquatic Macroinvertebrates

A few species of beetle larvae (especially whirligigs) are sometimes confused with dobsonfly, fishfly, or alderfly larvae because they may have similar fleshy filaments along the sides of the abdomen and may also have four hooks at the posterior. On beetle larvae with these characteristics, the four hooks come from a single short projection (point) instead of two hooks coming from two fleshy extensions like fishfly and dobsonfly larvae. In addition, beetle larvae do not have a single filamentous tail like alderflies.

Caddisfly larvae are sometimes mistaken for dobsonfly, fishfly, or alderfly larvae, but caddisfly larvae do not have fleshy filaments extending out from the sides of their abdomen and have only two abdominal hooks.

■ Dragonfly and Damselfly Larvae (Order *Odonata*)

Dragonflies and damselflies are common inhabitants of aquatic environments. They usually have a generation period of one year, but many may have life cycles of up to four years.

Dragonfly and damselfly larvae are usually found near aquatic vegetation or in tree root mats.

Dragonfly and damselfly larvae are distinguished by:
- large eyes.
- three pairs of long segmented legs (six legs total) on upper-middle section of body with two claws on each.

- large scooplike lower lip that covers much of the bottom of the head.
- no gills on the sides or underneath the abdomen.

Damselfly larvae (Suborder *Zygoptera*) can be distinguished by:

- a narrow body with three paddle-shaped tails (gills extending in a tripod formation).

spreadwinged damselfly larva

- long, spindly legs and a thin, narrow body.
- body length: ¼ inch to 2 ½ inches.

Dragonfly larvae (Suborder *Anisoptera*) can be distinguished by:
- oval or round abdomen that may end in five wedge-shaped extensions.
- body length: ¼ inch to 2 ½ inches.

Similar Aquatic Macroinvertebrates

Damselflies may be mistaken for mayflies because of the presence of three tails, but the tails of damselflies are broad, extend from the body in a tripod formation, and are fan shaped (remember this by thinking of a damsel fanning herself). Mayfly larvae have three (sometimes two) filamentous tails that extend from the body parallel to each other.

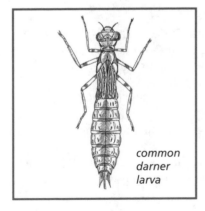

common darner larva

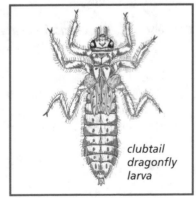

clubtail dragonfly larva

Dragonfly larvae are easily distinguishable by their oval or round (sometimes flattened) abdomen and their large, bulbous eyes.

■ **Aquatic Beetles** (Order *Coleoptera*)
Beetle larvae vary in shape, but they all have three pairs of segmented legs. The characteristics of each group of common aquatic beetle larvae are listed below.

☐ **Riffle beetles** (Family *Elmidae*):
Both adults and larvae are commonly encountered in streams and rivers. Adults are considered better indicators of water quality because they have been subjected to water conditions over a longer period.

Riffle beetle larvae are distinguishable by:
• an elongated body that has many segments and is relatively hard and stiff.
• three pairs of segmented legs (six legs total) on the middle section of the body.
• an opening at the posterior that has two tiny hooks and short hairs extending outward (hooks and hairs may be difficult to see).
• body length: up to ½ inch.

Adult riffle beetles can be distinguished by:
• small, oblong-shaped, beetlelike body.
• one pair of slender, segmented antennae.
• slow movement under water; they do not swim on the surface of the water.
• body length: ¹⁄₁₆ inch to ⅛ inch.

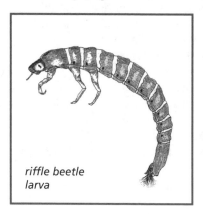

riffle beetle larva

adult riffle beetle

Similar Aquatic Macroinvertebrates

The most distinguishing characteristic of riffle beetle larvae is the hardened, stiff appearance of the entire body. Caddisfly larvae only have a hard covering over the first one, two, or three segments.

The most distinguishing characteristics of adult riffle beetles are their slow walking pace under water and their oval-shaped bodies. Long-toed water beetles look and act very similar to riffle beetles and should be included on Save Our Streams surveys.

Other adult beetles such as whirligigs and water pennies may occasionally be found while monitoring, but they are not used in SOS surveys because they are not dependent on oxygen in the stream. Whirligig beetles live on the surface of the water, usually swim frantically under water, and then pop back up to the surface. Their bodies are rounder (as seen from above) than riffle beetles'. Beetles that normally do not live under water will either die when submerged or rely on an air bubble that forms under their abdomen. In general, beetles that do not continually live in a stream are not comfortable under water.

☐ **Long-toed water beetles** (Family *Dryopidae*)
Adult long-toed water beetles are aquatic and look very similar to adult riffle beetles. They can be distinguished from one another by their club-shaped antennae, which are difficult to see. Because their characteristics are so similar, they should be included along with the riffle beetle adults on SOS survey forms. The larvae of long-toed water beetles are terrestrial and will not likely be found in streams.

☐ **Water pennies** (Family *Psephenidae*)
Only the larvae of water pennies are aquatic, although adults may be seen on rocks or reedy vegetation along the shoreline. Larvae are diskshaped and well adapted for clinging to rocks in current. They are often difficult to remove from surfaces.

Water penny larvae can be distinguished by:
- round (pennylike) body almost as wide as it is long.
- segmented platelike covering that conceals the head, legs, and gills (if present).
- three tiny pairs of segmented legs (six legs total).
- a body that often sticks flat to surfaces and looks like a tiny piece of leaf.
- their brown, black, or tan color.
- body length: up to ½ inch.

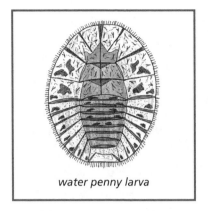

water penny larva

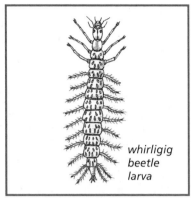

whirligig beetle larva

Similar Aquatic Macroinvertebrates

Water pennies are rarely confused with other aquatic macro-invertebrates because of their unique shape and the characteristic way the body appears to fuse to surfaces.

☐ **Whirligig beetles** (Family *Gyrinidae*)

Whirligig beetles are common stream inhabitants. The adults are good swimmers and are normally found on the surface in quiet pools. But because whirligig larvae are hard to find, they are not included in SOS surveys.

Whirligig beetle larvae can be distinguished by:

- pincerlike mouthparts.
- three pairs of segmented legs (six legs total) on the middle section of the body that end with tiny claws.
- filaments extending from the sides of the abdomen (may be difficult to see).
- an abdomen that ends with four hooks extending from one projection.
- no filamentous tails.
- body length: up to 1¼ inch.

Similar Aquatic Macroinvertebrates

The larvae of whirligig beetles resemble fishfly, alderfly, or dobsonfly larvae in that they have pincerlike mouthparts, tiny claws at the end of each leg, and filaments extending from the sides of the abdomen. Whirligig beetle larvae are different, however, in that the head and upper body tend to be narrower and the tail end is pointed with four hooks. Fishfly and dobsonfly larvae have two separate pairs of hooks on each side of a forked abdomen, and alderfly larvae have a single filamentous tail with no hooks.

☐ **Predaceous diving beetles** (Family *Dytiscidae*)
Adult predaceous diving beetles are common in slow-moving waters and are strong swimmers. They must regularly return to the surface to replenish their air supply. Because they are not dependent on oxygen dissolved in the water and are able to relocate easily, they are not useful indicators of water quality.

Larvae of predaceous diving beetles may occasionally be encountered in streams.

Predaceous diving beetle larvae are distinguished by:
• six jointed legs.
• a segmented body with a constriction or narrow collar behind the head.
• an abdomen that may have filaments extending from the sides and end of the abdomen, but does not have abdominal hooks.
• large crescent-shaped, pincerlike mouthparts.
• body length: ¼ inch to 2 ¾ inches

Similar Aquatic Macroinvertebrates

Larvae of predaceous beetles are not frequently found in riffle areas. Predaceous diving beetle larvae may be confused with alderfly, fishfly, and dobsonfly larvae because of the pincerlike jaws and large head. Predaceous diving beetle larvae have no abdominal hooks and commonly have a pair of filaments extending from the end of the abdomen. Alderfly larvae have single, branched, fila-

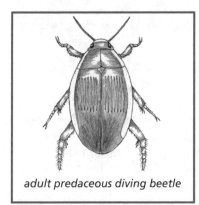

adult predaceous diving beetle

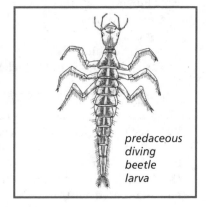

predaceous diving beetle larva

mentous tails extending straight back, and dobsonfly and fish-fly larvae have forked tails with two pairs of abdominal hooks. The lack of abdominal hooks differentiates predaceous diving beetle larvae from caddisfly larvae and other similar beetle larvae.

■ **True bugs** (Order *Hemiptera*)
True bugs are a diverse group of aquatic and semiaquatic macro-invertebrates. True bugs include water boatmen (Family *Corixidae*), water striders (Family *Gerridae*), marsh treaders (Family *Hydrometridae*), and others. Many of the semiaquatic true bugs are often seen skimming or walking along the surface of the water. Since these true bugs do not live under water and do not depend on oxygen in the water, and because they are also good swimmers that can relocate easily, they are not dependable indicators of water quality.

☐ **Water scorpions** (Family *Nepidae*)
Water scorpions are usually large (up to four inches) and narrow or ovalshaped (two main types) with three pairs of jointed legs. The front pair of legs has single hooks, which are modified for grasping. A long breathing tube formed by two filaments extends from the posterior and is the distinguishing feature of this family.

☐ **Giant water bugs** (Family *Belostomatidae*)
Giant water bugs may be large (up to three inches) and appear similar to beetles. Like water scorpions and creeping water bugs, they have three pairs of jointed legs. The front pair of legs has a single hook at the end. Giant water bugs are sometimes confused with creeping water bugs; however, creeping water bugs carry air bub-

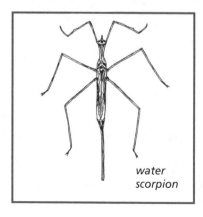

water scorpion

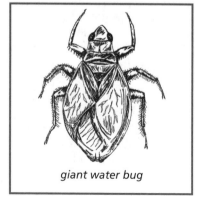

giant water bug

bles under their wings for breathing. Information regarding the pollution tolerance of creeping water bugs is limited.

■ Aquatic Caterpillars (Order *Lepidoptera*)

Aquatic caterpillars found in riffle areas usually have gill filaments covering their top and sides. Other aquatic caterpillars are often associated with aquatic vegetation in slow water and they lack gill filaments. The combination of six hooked legs and five pairs of caterpillarlike legs distinguishes this group. Aquatic caterpillars are not found frequently enough to be included on SOS surveys. They should be noted if found, however.

☐ Aquatic pyralid moths (Family *Pyralidae*)

The aquatic pyralid moths are the only family in *Lepidoptera* with completely aquatic stages found in streams. Larvae are caterpillarlike and can measure up to 1½ inch long. The midsection has three pairs of hooked legs. The abdomen has five pairs (located on abdominal segments three, six, and ten) of short, stubby prolegs.

aquatic pyralid moth larva

■ True Flies: Aquatic Flies and Midges (Order *Diptera*)

The larvae of this group are widely variable but can be distinguished from all other aquatic insects by the absence of segmented (jointed) legs on the midsection of the body. Larvae are usually wormlike and segmented. Organisms in *Diptera* are true flies. The families regularly encountered in moving streams are listed below.

☐ Crane flies (Family *Tipulidae*)

Crane fly larvae are fleshy, plump, and caterpillarlike. Most crane flies have one or two generations a year, but the aquatic stages can vary from six weeks to five years. Crane flies usually live in streambeds, are often found in leaf packs, and can be quite large. Close to 300 aquatic or semiaquatic species are recorded in North America.

Crane fly larvae can be distinguished by:
- a fleshy, plump, rounded, segmented body. The abdomen of some species is slightly flattened or flattens as it swims.
- a usually retracted head, giving the front end a rounded appearance.
- several extensions or fingerlike lobes on the posterior.
- a translucent, white, milky brown, or greenish body. Its digestive track (dark guts) can often be seen moving back and forth as it crawls.
- body length: ½ inch to 1 inch.

Similar Aquatic Macroinvertebrates

Crane fly larvae can be distinguished from other aquatic fly larvae by the presence of fleshy, fingerlike appendages extending from the posterior. In addition, crane fly larvae do not have the caterpillarlike legs that can be seen in watersnipe fly larvae or aquatic caterpillars, and the guts of crane fly larvae can often be seen inside the body.

☐ **Watersnipe Flies** (Family *Athericidae*)
Watersnipe fly larvae are predaceous, sensitive to pollution, and usually found in streams with good oxygen levels. Larvae can bite if disturbed.
   Watersnipe fly larvae are distinguished by:
- a cylindrical body that tapers into a conical shape at the head. The body is soft and fleshy, pale to greenish in color with many pairs of caterpillarlike legs on the underside.
- two hornlike tails with feathery hairs at the posterior.

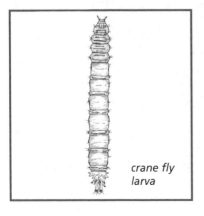

crane fly
larva

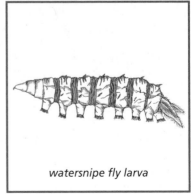

watersnipe fly larva

- tiny, soft pairs of fleshy filaments extending from the tops and sides of body segments.
- body length: ¼ inch to 1 inch.

Similar Aquatic Macroinvertebrates

Watersnipe fly larvae can be distinguished from other aquatic fly larvae and aquatic caterpillars by the presence of many caterpillar-like legs and the two feathery hornlike tails at the posterior. Dance flies may have caterpillarlike legs and two or more extensions from the posterior, but these extensions are shorter, blunted, and lack the branch hairs that make the tails of the watersnipe fly look feathery. Crane fly, horse fly, and deer fly larvae are distinguishable because they lack the caterpillarlike legs characteristic of water-snipe fly larvae. In addition, horse fly and deer fly larvae often have fleshy rings encircling their bodies.

☐ Black flies (Family *Simuliidae*)

Black fly larvae are fastened by their attachment disks (small suckers on the end of the abdomen) to the surface of rocks, sticks, or other debris in streams. The larvae can move by drifting downstream on silken threads that extend from the tip of the abdomen.
   Black fly larvae are distinguished by:

- a bulbous posterior, shaped like a bowling pin and ending with a tiny sucker.
- a segmented body (although difficult to see without magnification) and has distinct head.
- a usually black head; it's less often brown, tan, or green.
- one very tiny leglike appendage (proleg) located directly under the head (with magnification it looks like a small bump); otherwise, no legs are present.
- body length: up to ¼ inch.

Similar Aquatic Macroinvertebrates

The characteristics that distinguish the black fly larvae from other fly larvae or worms are the bulbous posterior (bowling pin shape) and dark head.

☐ Midges (Family *Chironomidae*)

Midges are a very large family with almost 2,000 species in North America. They have adapted very well to a wide variety of aquatic environments and may be found in all but the most degraded of

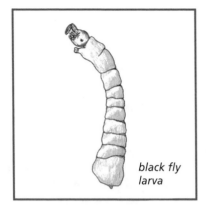

black fly larva

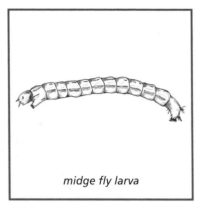

midge fly larva

aquatic conditions. They are often considered indicators of organic enrichment.

Midges can be distinguished by:

- their larvae, which usually have thin, slightly curved, segmented, inchwormlike bodies with distinct, often darkened heads. Generally, they are whitish olive to clear in color, but occasionally they are bright red.
- one pair of tiny, fleshy, unjointed prolegs below the head and one pair on the posterior (may be very small and hard to see).
- a tiny pair of filamentous tufts or extensions that sometimes appear on the posterior.
- their guts often appearing as a thin, dark line inside the body.
- body length: up to ¼ inch in streams (lake midges can be larger).

Similar Aquatic Macroinvertebrates

Midges are distinguishable from other aquatic fly larvae by their thin, uniformly wide, segmented bodies and the tiny pairs of fleshy legs, one pair behind the head and one under the end of the abdomen.

The following aquatic fly larvae do not appear on the SOS data form because they are not commonly found, although they may be encountered.

☐ **Dance flies** (Family *Empididae*)

Dance flies closely resemble watersnipe fly larvae, but they are generally smaller (up to ⅓ inch) and the extensions from the posterior are short and vary in number (there may be more than two).

dance fly larva

horse fly larva

In addition, these extensions do not have the branched filaments that give the extensions on the watersnipe fly a feathered look.

☐ **Horse and deer flies** (Family *Tabanidae*)
Horse and deer fly larvae found in streams usually are long (¾ inch to 1½ inch), cylindrical, and have a number of fleshy rings encircling them. They do not have legs, and their bodies are tapered or conical at both ends. If left undisturbed, a small breathing tube may be seen extending from one end.

☐ **Soldier flies** (Family *Stratiomyidae*)
Soldier fly larvae are occasionally encountered in streams. They have a distinct head, a wide, flat, segmented body, and are often covered with hairs or bristles. The body is usually stiff and has a hard skin. The tail end is tufted with many fine hairs.

soldier fly larva

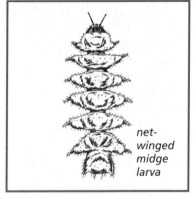

net-winged midge larva

☐ **Net-winged midge larvae** (Family *Blephariceridae*)

This group is usually only encountered in cold mountain streams and can be distinguished by the presence of six attachment disks (suckers) centrally located on the underside of body segments. The larvae are flattened from the top (wider than they are high) and have distinct constrictions, or waistlike indentations, between each of the seven body segments. Although superficially resembling sowbugs, net-winged midge larvae do not have segmented legs or long antennae.

Crustaceans: Class *Malacostraca*

■ **Crayfish** (Order *Decapdoa*)

Crayfish (also known as crawfish or crawdads) are common stream inhabitants, with about 350 species living in North America. The limited information available on crayfish life histories indicates that most species live for approximately two years, although certain species may live up to six or seven years. At certain times of the year, females may be observed with eggs or young clinging to the underside of their abdomens. They are often found hiding under rocks by day and foraging on stream bottoms at night. Crayfish grow by molting (shedding their shell). After crayfish have shed their hard covering, their new shells are very soft and they need to hide to avoid predators until their shells harden. Crayfish are considered keystone organisms in streams, as their presence is extraordinarily important and can provide enough energy to drive an entire ecological system.

Crayfish resemble small lobsters and can be distinguished by:

crayfish

- five pairs (unless broken off) of walking legs (including two large, lobster-like claws at the front).
- eyes that protrude from the body.
- a usually red, orange, brown, or dark color.
- body length: ½ inch to 5 inches.

Similar Aquatic Macroinvertebrates

Crayfish are not often confused with other aquatic macroinvertebrates and can easily be distinguished from freshwater shrimp by the presence of two lobsterlike claws.

■ Freshwater Shrimp (Order *Decapoda*)

Although occasionally encountered in riffle areas, freshwater shrimp are more common in slow-moving brackish or freshwater streams in coastal or lowland areas.

Freshwater shrimp can be distinguished by:
- five pairs of narrow walking legs (small claws on first two pairs), none enlarged like lobster claws.
- eyes that protrude from the body.
- a clear, milky, or light brown color.

Freshwater shrimp are similar in many ways to crayfish, but the former do not have large lobsterlike claws or expanded claw legs. Freshwater shrimp are often clear, milky, or light brown in color with a thinner shell than crayfish.

■ Scuds (Order *Amphipoda*)

Scuds (side swimmers) are most commonly found in water with an abundance of aquatic vegetation. They can be observed scooting around on their sides in collection dishes.

Scuds can be distinguished by:
- their shrimplike appearance, but they lack the large hard covering over the head and upper body.
- a white to clear body with many segments.

freshwater shrimp

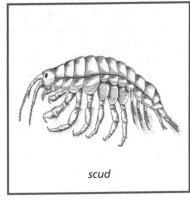

scud

- their laterally flattened (side to side) shape—taller than they are wide.
- two pairs of antennae.
- seven pairs of tiny legs.
- swimming rapidly on their sides (hence, the nickname "side swimmer").
- body length: ⅛ inch to ¼ inch.

Similar Aquatic Macroinvertebrates

Scuds are sometimes confused with sowbugs, but scuds are taller than they are wide and swim rapidly on their sides, while sowbugs have flattened, oblong bodies and crawl along surfaces. Scuds are also similar to freshwater shrimp. However, shrimp are more likely to be found in coastal and lowland areas, whereas scuds will be found inland.

■ Sowbugs (Order *Isopoda*)

Sowbugs, also known as aquatic pillbugs, are mostly terrestrial or marine, but approximately 130 freshwater species live in North America. Large numbers of sowbugs are often an indication of organic enrichment.

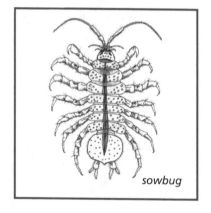

sowbug

Sowbugs can be distinguished by:

- dark brown or gray color, with an armorlike appearance.
- a dorsally flattened shape (top to bottom), much wider than they are tall.
- two pairs of antennae (one pair is usually much longer).
- their slow crawl over surfaces.
- body length: ¼ inch to ¾ inch.

Similar Aquatic Macroinvertebrates

Sowbugs are sometimes confused with scuds, but sowbugs are wider than they are tall. Sowbugs also walk slowly along surfaces.

Snails: Class *Gastropoda*

Snails possess a single shell that is usually coiled, although sometimes they are flattened and coneshaped, in which case they are called limpets. There are two distinct groups of snails that generally have different sensitivities to stream conditions.

■ **Gilled snails** (Subclass *Prosobranchia*)
These snails have gills and rely on oxygen in the water for respiration. Gills require that a thin surface layer is exposed for oxygen to pass through, and this layer may cause gilled snails to be more susceptible to chemical and physical alterations in stream quality.
Gilled snails are distinguished by:
• an operculum or platelike door that protects the opening of the shell and can be quickly closed to avoid predators.
• coiled shells that usually open on the right-hand side (dextral).
• body length: ¼ inch to 1 inch.
Note: The left or right coiling of the shell can be determined by holding the shell with its tip pointing up and with the opening of the shell facing you. If the opening is on your right-hand side then the shell is said to be right-handed, and the snail is likely a gilled snail.

■ **Lunged snails** (Subclass *Pulmonata*)
Pouched snails, pond snails, and other assorted snails and limpets are called lunged snails because they can trap pockets of air in their mantle cavity (the space between their shell and body) and obtain oxygen directly from the air. Because lunged snails can get

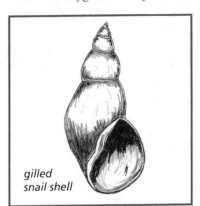

gilled snail shell

limpet shell

air from above the water's surface, they are not as sensitive to pollutants like organic matter.

Lunged snails are distinguished by:

- no platelike covering over the shell opening.
- a shell that spirals with the opening usually on the left side. The shell is either coiled in one plane, or is dome- or hat-shaped with no coils.
- body length: up to 2 inches.

Similar Aquatic Macroinvertebrates

Although snails are not often confused with other aquatic macro-invertebrates, it is important to distinguish whether the snail is gilled or has lungs. Gilled snails have a hard platelike cover over the shell opening, and identification may be made by the position of the opening. It is important to make sure the snail is alive (the shell is occupied) before counting it on the SOS Stream Quality Survey data form.

Clams and Mussels: Class *Bivalvia*

This class includes clams and mussels that live in most freshwater habitats and may be particularly abundant in certain streams. Although clams and mussels have a wide range of tolerances to pollution, with some species being very sensitive to water quality, habitat, and biological conditions, a number of species (especially clams) can tolerate somewhat degraded conditions.

Mussels have larval stages that are parasitic on specific fish species and are dependent on the host fish for dispersal within

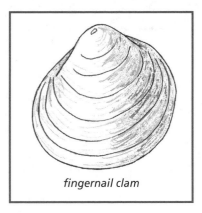

fingernail clam

unionid mussel

aquatic systems. As a result, problems such as barriers to fish movement, or the reactions of mussels or host fish to environmental conditions, may cause complex and variable responses in mussel populations. Because of their long life span and sensitivity to environmental change, most mussel species are good indicators of water quality.

Clams and mussels are distinguished by:
- two mirrored shells attached by an external hinge ligament.
- no eyes or distinct head.
- a fleshy body, foot, or two tubelike siphons that may extend from the shell when undisturbed and in water.
- body length: ⅛ inch to 5 inches.

Similar Aquatic Macroinvertebrates

Clams and mussels are rarely mistaken for other macroinvertebrates. "Dead" clams or mussels (empty shells) do not accurately reflect water quality because the shells can persist for long periods before breaking down, regardless of water conditions.

Generally, mussels are large (up to five inches) and have a flat, oblong shell, while freshwater clams are smaller (¾ inch) and are typically rounder. In addition, freshwater clams are usually symmetrical with the umbo (the highest point on the shell) equally distant from both ends. Mussel shells are usually lopsided with the umbo closer to one end.

Leeches: Class *Hirudinea*

Of the more than sixty-three species of freshwater leeches, approximately 25 percent are predaceous, not parasitic. In addition, only a few of those are parasitic on humans, and very rarely will you encounter these particular leeches in fast-moving water or riffle areas. All leeches feed on the fluids of other animals; however, many are scavengers of dead animals or feed on other invertebrates, and only a few are blood-sucking parasites. The suckers located at both ends of the body are used for attachment, feeding, and

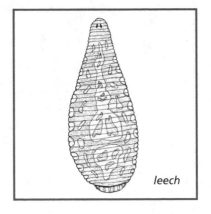

leech

locomotion. Some leeches can live for days without dissolved oxygen. Large numbers of leeches can indicate depleted dissolved oxygen levels in a stream.

Leeches can be distinguished by:

- a wormlike segmented body that is wider than it is high (the body is flattened from the top). the body is soft and slimy, and usually has a brown or gray pattern on top with suckers underneath at both ends (the sucker at one end is usually larger).
- graceful and quick swimming in an up-and-down motion. When confined in a collection dish, they may move by attaching suckers and slinking from end-to-end in an inchwormlike fashion.
- body length: ¼ inch to 2 inches.

Similar Aquatic Macroinvertebrates

Leeches can be distinguished from aquatic worms, planarians, or aquatic fly larvae by the presence of suckers at both ends of their body, their unique swimming style or end-to-end movement, and their usually flattened body.

Aquatic Worms: Class *Oligochaeta*

Aquatic worms are usually found in streams that contain much silt and organic debris. Some closely resemble terrestrial earthworms, while others are much narrower or even threadlike. Many aquatic worms can tolerate low levels of dissolved oxygen and may be found in large numbers in organically polluted streams.

Aquatic worms can be distinguished by:

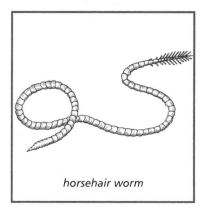

horsehair worm

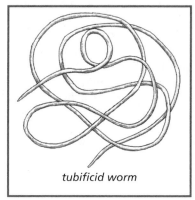

tubificid worm

- a red, tan, brown, or black body color.
- a cylindrical, thin (some threadlike), segmented body.
- short bristles or hairs (setae) that are sometimes present to help with movement (usually not visible).
- the absence of legs, a distinct head, or any mouthparts.
- stretching and pulling its body along in wormlike movements.
- body length: ¼ inch to 2 inches.

Similar Aquatic Macroinvertebrates

Can be distinguished from leeches, midges, and planarians by their long slender body and wormlike stretching and pulling movements.

Crane fly and watersnipe fly larvae can also look similar, but they have feathery or fingerlike extensions from the posterior and plumper caterpillarlike bodies. Watersnipe fly larvae also have caterpillarlike legs.

Planarians or Flatworms: Class *Turbellaria*

These small wormlike organisms are found in a variety of aquatic environments. Because of the difficulty in preserving these organisms, they have been less stud-
ied than other aquatic macroinvertebrates. Due to the inability to use planarians as an accurate indicator of water quality, they are not included on the SOS data form. In addition, they are not commonly found during SOS monitoring. Their presence, however, should be noted.

Planarians can be distinguished by:

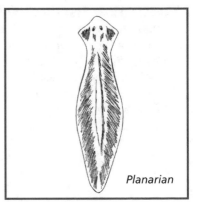

Planarian

- an unsegmented, soft, cigar-shaped, flattened body.
- a lobed or arrow-shaped head and distinct eyespots.
- having a body wider than it is high (flattened from the top).
- smooth, sliding movements along surfaces (rather than end-to-end like a leech or stretching part of the body and pulling the rest like a worm).
- body length: up to ¾ inch.

Appendix A
Izaak Walton League Volunteer Stream Monitoring Protocol

Surveying stream macroinvertebrates provides information about the health of your stream. Many stream-dwelling organisms are sensitive to changes in water quality. Their presence or absence can serve as an indicator of environmental conditions.

Before selecting a site to monitor, please follow these rules:

- Check with state and county agencies to make sure you are not disturbing a survey area used by government agencies (over-monitoring may harm the stream).
- Review Safety and Fun in Your Watershed (see page 62) and carefully prepare for your trip.
- Always contact local landowners before monitoring to make sure you are not trespassing.
- Ask for permission if you need to cross private land. Most landowners will give permission for your study, particularly if you offer to share your data; they may even want to help you conduct your survey.
- Collect samples upstream from bridge structures when possible. Bridges can have a variety of impacts on a stream, including discarded trash, glass, and petroleum or metal compounds from cars and salt from roads in the winter. Collecting samples upstream of the bridge gives more accurate data regarding the watershed.
- When sampling at point-source discharges, samples should be collected at least 100 yards downstream of the facility's outfall. Discharge permits contain allowances for "mixing zones" below discharge pipes. This is an area where some pollutants may not have been evenly diluted by stream flow. To obtain accurate information, samples should be collected below the mixing zone.

Monitoring should be conducted at the same station (location) each time you sample during the year. If you want to monitor several stations on your stream, make sure the stations are spaced no closer than a quarter mile apart. If the stations are spaced more closely, the monitoring activity may become the main impact on the water quality. If you want to monitor a one-mile segment of a stream, you can have a maximum of four monitoring locations.

Carefully record the location of your monitoring station on your Stream Quality Survey form (see page 60). Include roads, bridges, and significant landmarks. If you can locate your station on a topographic map, record your station according to longitude and latitude. By providing this information, you allow your station to be located from anywhere in the world and easily described to government officials and others. A free catalog of topographic maps is available from the U.S. Geological Survey at (800) USA-MAPS, or online at www.usgs.gov.

Things to Consider

If you are monitoring more than one station, begin monitoring downstream and move upstream. This will prevent macroinvertebrates disturbed by the first test from washing downstream and being captured in your net a second time. Each station survey should record only the organisms present at that particular location and time.

Monitoring should be conducted four to six times per year at each station. Monitor once each in the spring, summer, winter, and fall and at two other times during the year. These times may be after floods or other pollution events. The extra surveys, when compared with the regular seasonal surveys, will help to determine water quality impacts. Monitoring once each season will accurately record the yearly life cycle in the stream. Less frequent monitoring, while still useful, will not give the complete picture of stream life.

When scheduling monitoring events, remember that excessive monitoring can become the major threat to stream health. Each monitoring event disturbs the streambed and dislodges macroinvertebrates. In general, monitoring stations should have two months to recover from a monitoring event. It is crucial to the integrity of your data that you do not overmonitor your stations. There is some flexibility in this rule. For example, if an oil spill occurs, you might want to monitor your stream, even if you have done your six surveys for the year. The data you collect might be the only data available on the immediate impacts of the spill. Be sure to follow safety precautions from the Safety and Fun in Your Watershed fact sheet. Do not monitor streams where strong oil or chemical odors are present because they may indicate a health risk.

The methods described in these instructions are for use in wadable streams. To be wadable, the water level in the stream must not exceed the height of your knees. When planning monitoring sessions for younger people, please remember that knee height varies greatly between adults and children.

There are two sampling methods for collecting aquatic macroinvertebrates. The Muddy Bottom Sampling method is used in streams that do not have riffles—streambed features with cobble-sized stones (two to ten inches in diameter) where the water bubbles over the rocks. If your stream has riffles, please refer to the Rocky Bottom Sampling instructions.

Muddy Bottom Sampling

The Muddy Bottom Sampling Method is intended for volunteers sampling streams that do not have rocky bottoms or riffles. Muddy bottom streams are composed of muddy or sandy substrate, overhanging bank vegetation, and submerged woody and organic debris. This method enables sampling of streams where kick-seining techniques (see pages 52–53) do not yield the best representative sample of macroinvertebrates or allow easy collection from the most productive aquatic habitats.

Monitoring is conducted using an aquatic D-frame or dip net with $\frac{1}{32}$-inch mesh and a four-foot pole. The dip net is used to sample a wide variety of habitats and collect many different kinds of organisms.

*Equipment**

- One D-frame aquatic dip net with mesh of $\frac{1}{32}$ inch
- *Field Guide to Aquatic Macroinvertebrates*
- *A Guide to Aquatic Insects and Crustaceans*
- Stream Quality Survey data forms
- Fahrenheit thermometer
- Two small magnifier boxes (optional)
- Magnifying glass (optional)
- Plastic shallow pan
- Specimen jars or white ice cube trays for sorting organisms
- One screen-bottom bucket with a mesh of $\frac{1}{32}$ inch (optional)
- Tweezers or forceps (optional)
- Clipboard (optional)

*For information on how to obtain monitoring equipment and publications, please visit www.iwla.org or call (800) BUG-IWLA.

- White sheet or plastic trash bag (optional)
- Old sneakers or sandals that secure to your feet. Waders may be preferred in colder weather or where water is cloudy and one may desire more protection around the legs.

Before you begin monitoring, familiarize yourself with the four main habitats that can exist along muddy bottom streams: steep banks/vegetated margins, silty bottom with organic matter, woody debris with organic matter, and sand/rock/gravel/substrate. Search for these habitats along a fifty-foot section upstream from the monitoring station.

Following are simple descriptions of the habitat types and collection techniques for each habitat:

Steep banks/vegetated margins. This habitat is the area along the bank of the water body and consists of overhanging bank vegetation, plants living along the shoreline, and submerged root mats. Vegetated margins may be home to a diverse assemblage of dragonflies, damselflies, and other organisms. Move the dip net in a bottom-to-surface motion, jabbing at the bank to loosen organisms. Each scoop of the net should cover one foot of submerged area.

Silty bottom with organic matter. Silty substrates with organic matter can be found where the water is slow-moving and where there is overhanging vegetation or other sources of organic matter. They harbor burrowing organisms such as dragonflies or mayflies. Collect samples by moving the net forward (upstream) with a jabbing motion to dislodge the first few inches of organic layer.

Woody debris with organic matter. Woody debris consists of dead or living trees, roots, limbs, sticks, and other submerged organic matter. It is a very important habitat in slow-moving rivers and streams. The wood provides shelter from fish and other predators and traps organic particles that serve as food for the organisms.

To collect woody debris, approach the area from downstream and hold the net under the section of wood you wish to sample, such as a submerged log. Rub the bottom of the net frame along the surface of the log for a total surface area of one foot. You can also hold the net under the log and scrub the surface with a pot-scrubbing brush, washing the invertebrates into the net. It is also good to dislodge some of the bark, as organisms may be hiding underneath. You also can collect sticks, leaf litter, and rub roots attached to submerged logs. Be sure to thoroughly examine any small sticks you collect with your net before discarding them. There may be caddisflies, stoneflies, riffle beetles, and midges attached to the bark.

Sand/rock/gravel/substrate. In slow-moving streams, bottoms are generally composed of only sand or mud because the water is not fast enough to transport large rocks. Sometimes you may find a gravel bar located at a bend in the river. The bottom can be sampled by moving the net forward (upstream) with a jabbing motion to dislodge the first few inches of gravel, sand, or rocks. You may want to gently wash the gravel in your screen bottom bucket and then discard gravel in the river.

To provide for accuracy of collection and comparability of data from one station to another, take twenty scoops total from the different habitats combined. Each scoop involves a forward motion of one foot. The D-frame net is one foot wide, so one scoop equals one square foot being monitored.

Ideally, you should identify the location of all four main habitat types within about fifty feet of each monitoring station, and then collect the following number of scoops from each habitat:

- ten scoops from steep banks/vegetated margins
- three scoops from silty bottom with organic matter
- four scoops from woody debris with organic matter
- three scoops from sand/rock/gravel/substrate

If one of the habitat types is not present, divide the number of assigned scoops from that habitat between the other habitat types that are present. For example, if the stream does not have sand/rock/gravel/substrate, take one extra scoop from each of the other three habitat types. The most important thing is to have a total of twenty scoops and to make sure all habitat types in the monitoring area are represented.

If you have large rocks (greater than two inches in diameter), it is important to dislodge any burrowing organisms. To do this, hold the net on the downstream side of the rocks. In a one-square-foot area in front of the net, gently kick up the rocks with your toes or push them free with your fingers. This should dislodge burrowing organisms and allow them to wash into your net.

Each time you sample, sweep the mesh bottom of the D-frame net back and forth through the water (not allowing water to run over the top of the net) to rinse fine silt from the net. This will prevent a large amount of sediment and silt from collecting in the pan and clouding the water.

After collecting some samples, dump the net into a shallow white pan filled with a few inches of water. It is a good idea to do this every few scoops to avoid clogging the net. Clearing the net periodically also prevents having to sort too much debris at once.

Collect organisms from the net or pan and place them in similar groups as you go through the sample. This will make your identification quicker when you are ready to record results on your survey form. Plastic ice cube trays are helpful when identifying the sample. For example, put all organisms with two tails in one section and all organisms with three tails in another section. See the section on Identification in this fact sheet for more information.

Rocky Bottom Sampling

The Rocky Bottom Sampling method is intended for volunteers sampling streams that have rocky bottoms or riffles. A kick-seine net (a fine net with supporting poles on each side) is the best tool to use for collecting macroinvertebrates from rocky bottom streams. The League's Rocky Bottom Sampling method uses a kick-seine net that is three feet square with $1/16$- or $1/32$-inch mesh. While either size is adequate for obtaining accurate results, some state and local government agencies require use of the $1/32$-inch mesh. Both sizes capture the full range of macroinvertebrate species included in this monitoring method; however, the $1/32$-inch net will provide you with a larger sample because it captures smaller, younger organisms of each species.

*Equipment**
- Kick-seine net
- *Field Guide to Aquatic Macroinvertebrates*
- *A Guide to Aquatic Insects and Crustaceans*
- Stream Quality Survey data forms
- Fahrenheit thermometer
- Two small magnifier boxes (optional)
- Magnifying glass (optional)
- Shallow plastic pan
- Specimen jars or white ice cube trays for sorting organisms
- Tweezers or forceps (optional)
- White sheet or plastic trash bag (optional)
- Clipboard (optional)

---

*For information on how to obtain monitoring equipment and publications, please visit www.iwla.org or call (800) BUG-IWLA.

- Camera (optional)
- Squirt bottle, such as a well-rinsed liquid dish soap bottle or sports bottle (optional)
- Glass sample vial for your macroinvertebrate collection and 70 percent alcohol for specimen preservation (optional)
- Old sneakers or sandals that secure to your feet. Waders may be preferred in colder weather or where water is cloudy and one may desire more protection around their legs.

Select a shallow, fast-moving riffle with a depth of three to twelve inches and cobble-sized stones (two to ten inches or larger). Before entering the stream, record observations about riffle composition on the back of the stream quality data form (see page 60).

Place the kick-seine at the downstream edge of the riffle. Use rocks to secure the net tightly against the streambed so that no organisms escape under the net. Also, don't allow any water to flow over the top of the net; organisms can escape over the net. In addition, if water is flowing over the top of the net, the water level is too high for safe monitoring.

Monitor the streambed for a distance of three feet upstream of the kick-seine and across the width of the net. Firmly and thoroughly rub your hands over all rock surfaces to dislodge any attached insects. Carefully place all large rocks outside of your three-foot sampling area after you have rubbed off any macroinvertebrates. Stir up the bed with your hands and feet until the entire area has been searched. All exposed and detached organisms will be carried into the net. Then, for at least sixty seconds, use the toe of your shoe to jab the streambed with a shuffling motion toward the net. Disturb the first few inches of sediment to dislodge burrowing organisms.

Before removing the net, rub any rocks that you used to anchor the net to the stream bottom and remove the rocks from the bottom. Firmly grab the bottom of the net so that your sample does not fall from the net, and then remove it with a forward-scooping motion. The idea is to remove the net without allowing any insects to be washed under or off it.

Placing a white trash bag or white sheet under the net before separating the sample will catch any tiny organisms that may have crawled through the net. Use a watering can or spray bottle to periodically water your net. The organisms will stop moving as the net dries out. Occasionally wetting the net will cause the organisms to move, making them easier to spot. Watering the net is especially important on hot, dry days.

Place the net on a flat, bright area, out of direct sunlight. Using tweezers, a cotton swab (Q-tip), or your fingers, separate all the organisms from the net and place them in your collecting container, which should be half full of water. Sort organisms into similar groups as you separate your sample. Be sure to keep dobsonflies, fishflies, alderflies, dragonflies, damselflies, and so on separate from smaller organisms such as midge flies and black flies, as these smaller organisms may be eaten. Sorting the organisms will make identification quicker. White plastic ice cube trays are helpful when identifying the catch. For example, put all organisms with legs in one section and all organisms with no legs in another section. Any organism that moves, even if it looks like a worm, is part of the sample. Look closely, since most aquatic macroinvertebrates are only a fraction of an inch long.

Identification

Once organisms are collected through either the Muddy Bottom or Rocky Bottom sampling methods, they are sorted and identified using this book and *IWLA's Field Guide to Aquatic Macroinvertebrates*.

The Izaak Walton League's macroinvertebrate guides provide a general overview of the significance of macroinvertebrate types found across the United States. The composition of macroinvertebrate populations varies depending on local geography and geology. Try contacting your local environmental protection agency or universities for more information about the significance of locally found macroinvertebrates. Local experts might be able to share additional field guides that are specifically designed for your area.

Not all organisms in your stream are listed in the guides. For instance, macroinvertebrates such as whirligig beetles, water striders, and predaceous diving beetles are not included on the survey sheet. They are surface breathers and do not provide any indication of water quality.

When beginning your identification, ask yourself the following questions to identify an organism:
- How large is the organism?
- Is the body long and slender, round, or curved?
- Does the organism have any tails? How many?
- Does the organism have any antennae?
- Does the organism have legs? How many? Where?
- Is the body smooth and all one section, or is it segmented (with two or more distinct sections)?
- Does the organism have any gills (fluffy or platelike appendages)?

- Where are the gills located? Sides, back, underside, under its legs?
- Does it have pinching jaws like a beetle larvae?
- Are any legs or antennae missing because they were broken off in the net?
- What color is the organism?
- Does the organism swim underwater or remain on the surface?

When using the macroinvertebrate guides, remember to read the descriptions for each organism. The sizes of the organisms are also noted for reference; however, if you catch a young macroinvertebrate that has just hatched and has not yet reached full size, it may be smaller than indicated in the guides. Specimens can be put into magnifying boxes to ease identification. Volunteers also can call the IWLA help line at (800) BUG-IWLA.

After identifying your organisms, record your results on the IWLA Stream Quality Survey data form. Return the organisms to the stream after sampling is completed. Also include information relating to habitat and physical parameters of the stream in the survey on the back of the data form. Tabulate your results to determine the water quality using the instructions on the survey sheet. Use letters to indicate the number of each type of organism (A=1–9, B=10–99, C=100 or more). Add the number of letters in a column and multiply by the index value at the bottom. Add the subtotal for each column to arrive at your final stream rating.

You will notice that the letter (A, B, or C) does not affect the final rating score of excellent, good, fair, or poor. This is because the survey is based primarily on diversity, not the number of individual organisms found. The letters are valuable, however, because they document changes in populations over time. For instance, say your spring survey has only C's in the "pollution sensitive" column and only A's in the "pollution tolerant" category. In your summer survey, you find only A's in the sensitive range and C's in the tolerant range. You might conclude that overall water quality was declining because populations of the tolerant organisms are increasing (A to C) while those in the sensitive category are decreasing (C to A). You should monitor for an entire year to get a clear picture of your stream. Consult with local or state biologists to discuss your findings.

The League updates the sensitivity rankings for macroinvertebrates based on the most recent scientific research. To download a copy of the latest stream survey form, please visit our website at www.iwla.org.

Survey Data Form Questions

On the back of the survey data form there are a number of questions about the land and vegetation surrounding the stream. These questions help characterize the quality of stream habitat and its ability to support a healthy population of stream organisms. The land-use information also paints a picture of the stream for other people who might review your survey form. Guidelines for correctly answering these questions are given below. Record the answers based on the area that is upstream from your monitoring site; generally, you should record the data for the area that you can see. For land-use information, include uses for one mile upstream from your site or the section of stream you have adopted. If necessary, take a walk or consult a map for this information.

Fish water-quality indicators. The survey form asks if fish are present. Different fish have different tolerances to pollution. The types of fish present may indicate the type of water quality expected. You should not include fish that are stocked and do not survive through the winter or do not successfully reproduce from year to year. For example, trout are pollution-sensitive fish, but the presence of trout is not a good water quality indicator if the fish are stocked and only live for a few weeks. If you collect fish but don't recognize the type, write a description of the fish on the survey form or take a picture to use for later reference. You can find fish identification charts or experts to help with fish identification at local schools, agencies, libraries, or online.

Barriers to fish movement. The question concerning barriers to fish movement is important to consider because the absence of certain fish types in your stream section may be due to a dam or other large obstacle, not because of the water quality. Note on your survey form if the dam is upstream or downstream, and measure its distance from your survey site. Waterfalls should only be recorded if they are large enough that a fish could not reasonably jump over them or swim around them. Usually, waterfalls of a few feet or less are not impediments to upstream movement of fish.

Surface water appearance. Check more than one of the colors listed, but not all of them. Note if strange colors are present throughout the stream or only in one section, such as immediately below a discharge pipe or highway culvert.

Streambed deposit (bottom). Record the general appearance of the stream bottom. If the streambed does not have any apparent coating, you may note it as "other" and write in "normal."

Odor. Note any unusual odors. Odors may come from natural processes or may indicate potential water quality problems.

Stability of streambed. An unstable streambed can mean that soil is eroding from the bottom of the stream and may indicate water quality problems. When standing in the stream, determine how frequently the bed sinks beneath your feet.

Algae color. Algae feels slimy. You will notice it as you rub rocks during monitoring. A great deal of algae may indicate too many nutrients in the water. Sometimes more algae will appear in the spring after snowmelt releases extra nutrients into the stream. You should take note of the percent and type of algae present in the stream to make sure it is not increasing over time.

Algae located. Estimate the percentage of streambed that is covered by algae. Algae is often present in small quantities in healthy streams. Excess algae may indicate water quality problems.

Stream channel shade. Over the course of the day, estimate what percentage of the stream channel is shaded by streamside trees, shrubs, and grasses. Shading helps keep water cool and can be beneficial for aquatic life.

Streambank composition. Remember to look at both sides of the stream's banks. When questions ask for a percentage, use the information for both the left and right bank and combine values. For instance, if one side of the bank is completely bare from erosion while the other side is well vegetated, you should record the percent of bank coverage as 50 percent.

When recording total percentages of shrubs, grasses, and trees, you should look at both sides of the bank. If one side has artificial structures such as rock riprap or concrete, however you will have to account for such ground cover. For instance, if the left side of the bank is not vegetated, you cannot have more than 50 percent of shrubs, grasses, and trees total when those values are added together.

Streambank erosion. Again, looking at both sides of the bank, determine the percentage of soil erosion.

Riffle composition. This question refers to the three-by-three-foot area of stream sampled for rocky bottom sampling techniques with a kick-seine net. Do not fill out this question when using the muddy bottom sampling technique.

If you used a kick-seine to conduct the Rocky Bottom Sampling Method, answer this question before you disturb the site. The organisms you collect are most abundant in riffles composed of predominantly cobble-sized stones (more than 70 percent cobbles is a good riffle habitat). Start with the largest rocks first when recording bed composition. If you don't have any boulders (rocks larger than ten inches), record cobble-sized stones and continue until your percentages equal 100 percent. A typical riffle in a medium-gradient stream might be recorded as 5 percent boulders, 65 percent cobbles, 15 percent gravel, 10 percent sand, and 5 percent silt. Ranges are given on the survey form for the rock sizes. For the smaller rock sizes, remember that silt feels like talcum powder and sand feels gritty. If your riffle had 40 percent silt, 10 percent gravel, and no cobbles, you should either find another station to monitor or switch to the Muddy Bottom Sampling Method.

Land uses in the watershed. The survey form asks if land-use impacts are high (H), moderate (M), slight (S), or none (N). Although these questions are somewhat subjective, determining the impact is easy and straightforward. Note "H" for a land use if it comprises the majority of land in the watershed and is polluting the stream, such as a stream traveling through land that is being strip-mined for coal. Mark "H" if the land use has a severe impact on stream quality even though the land use does not utilize a great deal of land, such as a construction site that has caused the stream to be full of silt. Note "M" if the land use is definitely contributing to stream degradation, but is not the major cause for degradation (or is one of many causes). For example, parking lot runoff and trash from a shopping mall may contribute significantly to stream pollution, but they may not be the only causes of stream degradation. Note "S" for a land use if its impacts only slightly pollute the stream. For example, although a farm may be present, good farming practices and conservation measures may mean the pollution impact is negligible. If the land use is present but causing no pollution, write "N" for none. If the land use is not present, do not write anything. Also, you should take the time to drive or walk through your watershed before filling out this section to determine if these land uses are present and impacting the stream.

When considering land use as the controlling factor in stream quality, look not just at the area visible from the stream, but at all the land draining to the stream—the watershed. If the stream collects water from an intensely developed urban or agricultural area, do not be surprised if no organisms are found. Should this be the case, consider visiting a forested stream of the same size in the same watershed for sampling comparison. You might be surprised at the different types of organisms you find.

You can identify a pollution source by sampling the stream at quarter-mile intervals upstream from the initial sampling point (where a pollution impact is suspected) until quality improves. The pollution sources should be identified somewhere between the point where degraded conditions were first found and the point where water quality improves.

Comments. Use this space to record observations that are not noted elsewhere on the data form. This may include current and potential future threats to the stream's health.

Stream Problems and Their Effects on Stream Organisms

1. *Physical problems* may include excessive sediment from erosion, street runoff, or discharge pipes. Sediment can create poor riffle characteristics, contribute to excessive flooding, reduce flow, change water temperature, and smother aquatic life. The result is usually a reduction in the number of macroinvertebrates in the study area.
2. *Organic pollution* is from excessive human or livestock wastes or high nutrient enrichment from farm or yard runoff. The result is usually a reduction in the diversity of insects.
3. *Toxic pollution* includes chemical pollutants such as chlorine, acids, metals, pesticides, and oil. The result is usually a reduction in the number of insects.

OBSERVATION	ANALYSIS
High diversity, high numbers, many sensitive species such as stoneflies, caddisflies, and mayflies	No problem, good water quality
High diversity, low numbers	Possibly due to poor habitat conditions
Low diversity, high numbers	Organic pollution (nutrient enrichment) or sedimentation; excessive algal growth resulting from nutrient enrichment
Low diversity, low numbers, or no bugs but the stream appears clean	Toxic pollution (e.g., chlorine, acids, heavy metals, oil, herbicides, insecticides)

Appendix B

THE IZAAK WALTON LEAGUE OF AMERICA
Save Our Streams
Stream Quality Survey

Date _____
Time _____
Name _____

Please refer to the Izaak Walton League's volunteer stream monitoring protocol and identification guides to learn how to complete this form. Please use the League's *Field Guide to Aquatic Macroinvertebrates* to complete portions of this stream quality survey form. For assistance, please call (800) BUG-IWLA or send an e-mail to sos@iwla.org.

Stream _____ Station # _____ County/City _____

Location _____

Weather Conditions (last 72 hours) _____

Water temperature_____ F°? C°? Avg. stream width _____ ft. Avg. stream depth _____ ft. Flow rate _____
(above or below average)

Rocky Bottom Sampling
Before sampling, record riffle composition on the back of this form. Take 3 samples in the same riffle area, fill out this form, and keep the highest scoring sample for your records. To help track the number of samples you have collected, check one of the boxes below:

☐ Sample 1   ☐ Sample 2   ☐ Sample 3   ☐ Is this your highest score sample?

Muddy Bottom Sampling
Record the total number scoops taken from each habitat type and provide details to best describe the specific habitat on the lines below:

☐ Steep bank/vegetated margin _____

☐Woody debris with organic matter _____

☐ Rock/gravel/sand substrate _____

☐ Silty bottom with organic matter _____

Macroinvertebrate Count
Consult the stream monitoring instructions on how to conduct the macroinvertebrate count. Use letter codes (A = 1-9, B = 10-99, C = 100 or more) to record the numbers of organisms. Add up the number of organism types (or number of letters) found under each category (sensitive, less sensitive, etc.) and multiply by the indicated index value. Although A, B, and C ratings do not contribute to the water quality rating, the letters track the population size in each category to see how the macroinvertebrate community changes over time.

SENSITIVE	LESS SENSITIVE		TOLERANT
___ Caddisflies (except net spinners)	___ Dobsonflies	___ Alderflies	___ Aquatic worms
___ Mayflies	___ Fishflies	___ Crayfish	___ Black flies
___ Stoneflies	___ Common	___ Scuds	___ Midge flies
___ Water snipe flies	net spinning	___ Aquatic	___ Leeches
___ Riffle beetles	Caddisflies	sowbugs	___ Lunged snails
___ Water pennies	___ Crane flies	___ Clams	
___ Gilled snails	___ Damselflies	___ Mussels	
	___ Dragonflies		
___ # of letters multiplied by 3 =___	___ # of letters multiplied by 2 =___		___ # of letters multiplied by 1 =___
Now add the three totals from each column for your stream's index value. Total index value = _____			

Compare the final index value to the following ranges of numbers to determine the water quality of the stream sample site.

Water Quality Rating

_____ Excellent (> 22)   _____ Good (17-22)   _____ Fair (11-16)   _____ Poor (< 11)

Fish Populations:	Barriers to fish movement:	Refer to the IWLA monitoring instructions to learn how to score these stream characteristics	
☐ scattered individuals ☐ scattered schools ☐ trout ☐ bass ☐ catfish ☐ carp ☐ other	☐ beaver dams ☐ man-made dams ☐ waterfalls (> 1 ft.) ☐ other ☐ none		

Surface water appearance:	Stream bed deposit (bottom):	Odor:	Stability of stream bed:
☐ clear ☐ clear, but tea-colored ☐ colored sheen (oily) ☐ foamy ☐ milky ☐ muddy ☐ black ☐ grey ☐ other _____	☐ grey ☐ orange/red ☐ yellow ☐ black ☐ brown ☐ silt ☐ sand ☐ other _____	☐ rotten eggs ☐ musky ☐ oil ☐ sewage ☐ other _____ ☐ none	Bed sinks beneath your feet in: ☐ no spots ☐ a few spots ☐ many spots
		Algae color: ☐ light green ☐ dark green ☐ brown coated ☐ matted on stream bed ☐ hairy	**Algae located:** ☐ everywhere ☐ in spots _____ % of bed covered

Stream channel shade:	Stream bank composition (=100%):	Stream bank erosion:	Riffle composition (=100%)
☐ > 80% excellent ☐ 50%-80% high ☐ 20%-49% moderate ☐ < 20% almost none	_____ % trees _____ % shrubs _____ % grass _____ % bare soil _____ % rocks _____ % other	☐ > 80% severe ☐ 50%-80% high ☐ 20%-49% moderate ☐ < 20% slight	_____ % silt (mud) _____ % sand (1/16" – ¼" grains) _____ % gravel (1/4" – 2" stones) _____ % cobbles (2" – 10" stones) _____ % boulders (> 10" stones)

Land uses in the watershed (upstream and surrounding sampling site):
Indicate whether the following land uses have a high (H), moderate (M), slight (S), or none (N) potential impact to the quality of your stream.

___ Oil & gas drilling	___ Urban uses (parking lots, highways, etc.)	___ Agriculture (type:_____)
___ Housing developments	___ Sanitary landfill	___ Trash dump
___ Forestry	___ Active construction	___ Fields
___ Logging	___ Mining (type: _____)	___ Other _____

Comments: Indicate the current and potential future threats to the stream's health and attach additional pages or photographs to better describe the condition of the stream.

....

....

....

IZAAK WALTON LEAGUE OF AMERICA ● 707 Conservation Lane ● Gaithersburg, MD 20878 ● 301-548-0150

For assistance, please call **(800) BUG-IWLA** or send an e-mail to **sos@iwla.org.**

Appendix C
Safety and Fun in Your Watershed

There are several important things to remember when you are working outside. If you follow these safety tips, you will have a fun and enjoyable experience.

Before You Go

Remember to tell a friend or relative the date, time, and location of your watershed activity. Work with a partner so that if you are injured, someone can go for help.

Find the phone number and location of the nearest medical center to your work site. Carry a cellular phone with you and note the location of a pay phone. Remember that cell phones do not always work in rural areas, so do not rely on them at all times.

Bring a first-aid kit that includes these items:

- Adhesive and cloth bandages
- Antiseptic spray or ointments
- Surgical tape
- Hydrogen peroxide
- Tweezers
- Cotton balls
- Aspirin or nonaspirin pain reliever
- Bee sting neutralizers

Review safety rules and tips with everyone in your work group before each outdoor project.

Safety Rules

The League recommends that groups never get into a stream when the water is at flood stage or is flowing much more swiftly than normal. It is better to delay monitoring or cleanup projects than to risk personal harm. Water should always be below the knees of the people who will be in the water. Remember that the knee level of children may be much lower than the knee level of adults. Avoid steep and slippery banks.

When in contact with water, keep your hands away from your eyes and mouth, as not all pollution can be seen or smelled, and water-borne diseases are often transferred by way of eyes and mouth. Always wash your hands thoroughly with soap and water after being in contact with stream or river water. You may also want to bring antibacterial hand gel to the field site for use immediately after water contact.

If the water is posted as unsafe for human contact or appears to be severely polluted, (strong smell of sewage or chemicals, unusual colors, lots of dead fish) do not touch the water. If these signs of severe pollution are not present, but you are unsure of conditions or would like additional protection, take the following precautions:

- Wear rubber boots high enough to keep water from contacting your skin.
- Wear heavy rubber gloves that go up to your shoulders (available at most automotive supply stores). Surgical gloves will not work—they can be punctured easily by snags or sharp objects, and they are not long enough to protect your arms.
- Wear a protective covering for your mouth such as a painter's mask (available at most drugstores or hardware stores). You can get sick if you breathe in vapors from sewage-contaminated water.
- Report any pollution problems to your state's water regulatory agency.

Other Areas of Concern

Snakes. Snakes can be a concern when you are in an aquatic environment, especially slow-moving waters with overhanging vegetation. To avoid an encounter with a snake, observe the following rules:

- Check rocks, logs, and stubs for snakes. Snakes must get out of the water to dry their skin. They will lie on flat surfaces exposed to sunlight.
- If you have to approach the water through high grass, thump the ground in front of you with a stick. Snakes will feel the vibrations and move away. Snakes are deaf and respond only to vibrations.
- If you come upon a snake at close range, simply move away. The snake probably will leave the area when it no longer perceives you as a threat. Remember, you are much bigger than the snake,

and it is more afraid of you than you are of it. Allow the snake a chance to back off, and it usually will.

- Most snakes associated with aquatic environments are not poisonous; however, because it's difficult to distinguish between poisonous and nonpoisonous snakes without getting too close, the best advice is to stay away from them all. If a snake bite does occur, follow these simple steps:
  1. Elevate the bitten area. Do not apply ice or a tourniquet to the wound. Do not cut the wound open or attempt to suck out the venom.
  2. Remain calm. Take a few deep breaths and keep movement to a minimum. Walk calmly to your vehicle and have your partner carry your equipment.
  3. Remove all watches and jewelry if bitten on the hand or arm. Snake venom will cause the bitten area to swell.
  4. Seek immediate medical attention.

Insects. If you are allergic to any insects, bring your antidotes or medicines. Ask other members of your group about their allergies before you go to the site. If a volunteer gets an insect bite that swells up to an unusual size or has severe redness, seek medical attention immediately.

Many people have concerns about West Nile virus. Female mosquitoes transmit the virus primarily among birds. Occasionally, mosquitoes transfer the virus from birds to humans, most of whom experience no symptoms. About one in five infected people develop West Nile fever, which resembles the flu. Infections can be fatal in people with weak immune systems, but this is rare. To avoid mosquito bites, wear long sleeves and pants. Avoid areas of standing water during dawn and dusk, when mosquito activity is at its peak. Consider using mosquito repellants that contain DEET. Do not spray DEET underneath clothes. For more information on West Nile virus, see the U.S. Environmental Protection Agency fact sheet "Wetlands and West Nile Virus" online at www.epa.gov/owow/wetlands/facts/WestNile.pdf, or contact the Izaak Walton League.

Ticks. Ticks are prevalent in grassy or woody areas. It is important for volunteers to check their bodies for ticks. Feel along the scalp for any loosely attached bumps. If it is a tick, do not pull it out. Yanking the tick might cause an infection if its head remains in the scalp. Grasp the tick with tweezers and gently twist it counterclockwise for several rotations until the tick is free. Swab the area with hydrogen peroxide to clean the area. If you want to kill the tick, burn it with a match or suffocate it with nail polish or petroleum jelly after it has been removed from the skin.

One type of tick, called a deer tick, can carry a serious illness called Lyme disease. Deer ticks resemble common ticks except they are much smaller (only a few millimeters across). Symptoms of Lyme disease include chills, malaise, and fever. Often the first sign of Lyme disease is a bullseye mark on the skin, but this is not always present. Treatment requires a shot of prescribed antibiotics. If not treated, this disease can remain in your body for a lifetime. If you exhibit any of the symptoms, it is recommended that you see your doctor and ask for a Lyme disease test.

Alligators and turtles. In southern states, you may encounter alligators and large aquatic turtles. These animals are not dangerous if left alone. Alligators under eighteen inches long are juveniles and may be near their mothers. Female alligators are very protective and may be dangerous. If you see alligators, leave the area immediately. Snapping turtles and soft-shelled turtles usually will move out of an area if the water is disturbed. Although turtles are not poisonous, treat a turtle bite with the same care as a snake bite.

Bears. Black bears and grizzly bears live in forested areas around the United States. Black bear encounters are more prevalent in the eastern U.S., while grizzlies may be encountered in the Northwest.

- When in an area with the potential for bear encounters, make sure you stay with a group of people and make noise to alert the bears of your presence.
- If you see a bear and it does not see you, quickly leave the area while keeping your distance from the bear, giving it plenty of room to escape should you startle it.
- If you encounter a bear and it sees you, do not run. You cannot outrun a bear. Stay calm and slowly back away from the bear. Look for an escape route that gives the bear plenty of space; try to stay out of its "comfort zone."
- Climbing trees to escape is a common suggestion, but be aware that many bears can follow you up a tree.
- If a bear should charge you, do not run. Drop to the ground and cover your head, face, and neck with your arms for protection. Lie motionless and give the bear time to leave the area. If you feel the attack is predatory, disregard the above strategy and fight back with everything you have.
- Never go near a cub because the mother bear is always nearby and will become very aggressive in trying to protect her young.

Glossary

Abdomen. The major body region located at the posterior.

Abdominal hooks. Variable numbers of hooks often located at the extreme posterior of many macroinvertebrates. Under most circumstances, these hooks may be difficult to see. To determine their presence and number, grasp the specimen from above along the sides of the head and upper body and slowly slide the tip (end) of the abdomen over the surface of the back of your other hand. Any hooks present will usually grab onto your skin surface.

Anterior. The front or part of the body closest to the head.

Appendage. Any extension or outgrowth from the body. Appendages are most commonly paired with one on each side of the body.

Aquatic macroinvertebrates. Organisms that live in water for all or part of their life, do not have a backbone, and are large enough to be seen without the aid of a microscope.

Benthic. To live in the benthos or stream bottom.

Dextral. Coiled shells that open on the right-hand side. The left or right coiling of the shell can be determined by holding the shell with its tip pointing up and with the opening of the shell facing you.

Dichotomous key. A key that enables one to identify an organism based on a series of options that consist of pairs of statements with opposite characteristics from which to choose.

Elongated. Refers to a body shape longer than it is wide.

Functional feeding groups. Categories in which aquatic macroinvertebrates can be divided based on their feeding patterns.

Generation. One complete life cycle.

Gills. Breathing apparatuses for aquatic organisms. May appear as hairs, tufts, or plates.

Hatch. In this book, hatch refers to a period when insects are rising off the water, changing from an aquatic to a terrestrial form. This term also refers to the time when the larva releases itself from the egg.

International Code of Zoological Nomenclature. The ranking system by which scientists have divided the living world into groups. These divisions progress from general (kingdom) to more specific (species).

Jointed appendage. Composed of several usually stiff sections that are held together and are often flexible or movable at the attachment point.

Mantle cavity. In a mollusk, the space between its shell and body.

Operculum. A platelike door that protects the opening of a snail's shell and can be quickly closed to avoid predators.

Parasitic. One organism living off another organism, either prior to killing it or without ever killing it.

Posterior. The back end of the body.

Proleg. A fleshy leg on some insect larvae; will not occur on the adult.

Predaceous. An organism that attacks, kills, and feeds off other organisms.

Segmented. Divided into similar and repeated units.

Sinistral. Left-handed; opening to the left.

Taxonomic level. The classification level of a living thing within the International Code of Zoological Nomenclature.

Thorax. The section of anthropods (insects, crustaceans, spiders, etc.) located behind the head and in front of the abdomen. The legs and wings attach to the thorax segments.

Umbo. On mollusks, the bump or highest part of the domed shell. The umbo is usually located close to the hinge attachment of the shell.

Bibliography

Bouchard, R. W., Jr., 2004. *Guide to Aquatic Macroinvertebrates of the Upper Midwest.* St. Paul: Water Resources Center, University of Minnesota.

Burch, J. B., 1982. *Freshwater Snails (Mollusca Gastropoda) of North America.* Cincinnati: U.S. EPA, Office of Research and Development. EPA 600/3-82/026. NTIS #PB82-207168.

Cummins, K. W., and M. A. Wilzbach, 1985. *Field Procedures for Analysis of Functional Feeding Groups of Stream Macroinvertebrates.* Frostburg: University of Maryland. ASIN B0071F3A4.

Edmunds, G. F., Jr., S. L. Jensen and L. Berner, 1976. *The Mayflies of North and Central America.* Minneapolis: University of Minnesota Press.

Klemm, D. J., 1985. *A Guide to Freshwater Annelida (Polychaeta, Naidid and Tubificid Oligochaeta and Hirudinea) of North America.* Dubuque, Ia: Kendall/Hunt Publishing Company.

Klemm, D. J., P. A. Lewis, F. Fulk, J. M. Lazorchak, 1990. *Macroinvertebrate Field and Laboratory Methods for Evaluating the Biological Integrity of Surface Water.* Cincinnati: U.S. EPA, Office of Research and Development. EPA/600/4-90/030. NTIS #PB91-171363.

Lehmkuhl, D., 1979. *How to Know the Aquatic Insects.* Dubuque, Ia: Picture Key Nature Series, William C. Brown, Co.

McCafferty W. P., 1983/1998. *Aquatic Entomology: A Fishermen's and Ecologists' Illustrated Guide to Insects and Their Relatives.* Boston: Jones and Bartlett Publishers, Inc. (800) 832-0034.

Merritt, R. W. and K. W. Cummins (eds), 1996. *An Introduction to the Aquatic Insects of North America.* Third edition. Dubuque, Ia: Kendall/Hunt Publishing Company.

Needham, J. G. and P. R. Needham, 1988. *A Guide to the Study of Freshwater Biology.* Fifth edition. San Francisco: Holden-Day, Inc.

Peckarsky, B. L., et al., 1990. *Freshwater Macroinvertebrates of North America.* Ithaca, N.Y.: Cornell University Press.

Pennak, R. W., 1989. *Freshwater Invertebrates of the United States: Protozoa to Mollusca*. Third edition. Somerset, N.J.: John Wiley and Sons, Inc.

Stewart, K. W. and B. P. Stark, 1988. *Nymphs of North America Stonefly Genera (Plecoptera)*. Hyattsville, Md.: Thomas Say Foundation Series, Volume 12. Entomological Society of America.

Thorp, J. H., and A. P. Covich, ed., 2001. *Ecology and Classification of North American Freshwater Invertebrates*. Second edition. San Diego: Academic Press, Harcourt Brace Jovanovich Publishers.

University of Minnesota, Water Resources Center. St. Paul, Minnesota. http://wrc.coafes.umn.edu/vsmp/education.htm.

Voshell, J. R., Jr., 2002. *A Guide to Common Freshwater Invertebrates of North America*. Blacksburg, Va.: The McDonald & Woodward Publishing Company.

Weiderholm, T., ed., 1983. *Chironomidae of the Holarctic Region, Keys and Diagnoses*. Part 1: Larvae. Entomologica Scandinavica. Supplement 19:1–457. Sandby, Sweden: Scandinavian Entomology Co.

Wiggins, G. B., 1995. *Larvae of the North America Caddisfly Genera (Trichoptera)*. Second edition. Toronto, Ontario: University of Toronto Press.

Additional Izaak Walton League Resources

Watershed Stewardship Action Kit
The Watershed Stewardship Action Kit is designed for volunteers, students, and landowners who want to take action toward environmental conservation in their communities. The kit covers watershed ecology, water quality problems, and actions that individuals and groups can take to conserve watersheds. Educational fact sheets address stream and wetland ecology, water quality monitoring, and federal regulations. Action fact sheets teach readers to fundraise, organize watershed cleanups, reduce water usage at home, survey watersheds, and monitor water quality. This publication includes the instructions and data form for the Izaak Walton League's biological stream monitoring method. Use this resource to start your own watershed stewardship projects or to teach others about the importance of water conservation.

A Handbook for Stream Enhancement and Stewardship
This resource is intended to help citizens, communities, and governments implement environmentally sound, cost effective stream corridor stewardship programs. It is written in clear, accessible language and consolidates a wealth of information into a single, manageable volume. It provides a solid foundation by which volunteers can become informed observers, advocates, and organizers of stream enhancement programs.

Hands-on Save Our Streams: Science Projects Guide for Students
This student-focused guide contains project ideas, monitoring instructions, data forms, and information about stream ecology. It takes students through the steps to plan a successful science fair or community project. This book is recommended for grades six through twelve.

Save Our Streams Volunteer Trainer's Handbook
This publication is a 110-page, three-ring-binder handbook for coordinating a stream biological monitoring program. It includes an overview of steps for designing a monitoring network; setting project goals; enlisting and training volunteers; collecting, managing, and using stream data; budgeting; and fundraising. Appendixes include monitoring instructions, data forms, a macroinvertebrate identification card, and an extensive bibliography. Quantities are limited. ·

A Volunteer Monitor's Field Guide to Aquatic Macroinvertebrates
This handy reference tool is designed to help volunteer monitors identify aquatic macroinvertebrates when conducting water quality surveys. The laminated brochure is convenient and durable for outdoor use. The diagrams of the macroinvertebrate larvae and adults are grouped by biological type and display common features that characterize each. Symbols indicate the relative pollution-sensitivity categories (sensitive, less sensitive, and tolerant) based on the general Save Our Streams classification system. Diagrams are accompanied by descriptions for easy and accurate identification in the field.

Handbook for Wetlands Conservation and Sustainability,
Second Edition
This handbook explains wetland ecology, functions, and values. It provides tips for organizing your community to monitor, conserve, and restore local wetlands. It includes wetland definitions, monitoring instructions, project ideas, regulatory avenues for wetland protection, case studies, and an updated and extensive resource section.

Unlocking the Secrets of America's Wetlands
This is an introductory guide to wetlands. It helps interested citizens understand wetland ecology and why these valuable ecosystems are important for clean water, wildlife habitat, fisheries, and more. This is a good publication for students.

SOS for America's Streams: A Guide to Water Quality Monitoring
This 28-minute video demonstrates biological stream monitoring methods, macroinvertebrate identification techniques, and how to

adopt a stream. Great for training volunteers or introducing schools or community groups to monitoring.

Restoring America's Streams

This 28-minute video shows how to become a "stream doctor" and cure sick streams. The video explains stream processes and causes of stream instability. It demonstrates techniques for restoring streams using native vegetation and features case studies of successful projects.

Wetlands Stewardship: A Call to Action

This 28-minute video serves as a companion to the *Handbook for Wetlands Conservation and Sustainability*. The video can be used to motivate citizens, educators, planners, government representatives, business leaders, and students to participate in the conservation of our nation's wetland resources. The video demonstrates the importance of wetlands to the environment and shows activities that have been initiated in communities across the country.

To order these Izaak Walton League of America publications and videos, please contact:

McDonald & Woodward Publishing Company
431-B East College Street
Granville, Ohio 43023
(800) 233-8787 (voice)
(740) 321-1141 (fax)
mwpubco@mwpubco.com

A more detailed listing of resources and contacts is available on our website at www.iwla.org. Resources include books, videos, websites, contacts, and other materials that provide additional information about watershed issues and conservation.

Index